Cottages & Conversions
at home and abroad

With love to Lionel
a fellow "converter"
from June (Field)

Cottages & Conversions
at home and abroad

June Field FRSA

John Bartholomew
Edinburgh

Other books by the same author:
The Ordinary Man's Guide to Collecting Antiques
Collecting Georgian and Victorian Crafts
Creative Patchwork

© June Field FRSA 1973
First published 1973
by John Bartholomew and Son Ltd.
12 Duncan Street, Edinburgh EH9 1TA
Also at 216 High Street, Bromley BR1 1PW
ISBN 0 85152 920 8

Designed and edited by Youé and Spooner Ltd.

Printed in Great Britain by
Cox & Wyman Ltd, London, Fakenham and Reading

contents

introduction

When I first started writing this book, I thought I had taken on an almost impossible task. There were the cottages and conversions I had come across over the years as my interest in property increased, but how would I hear of fresh ones? Would there be enough information to fill a book?

I need not have worried. The whole thing, like Topsy, just grew. The magic words "cottages and conversions" drew material from sources all over Britain and Europe – estate agents, architects, interior designers and decorators, builders, photographers, cottage owners and people with friends who lived in "the most unusual conversion you have ever seen". They nearly all lived up to expectation, and they get my deepest appreciation and thanks.

I soon began to realise the enormous interest that people all over the world had in their houses, an interest that was not confined to their own homes, but which extended to other people's too. The fascination of collecting houses, or rather ideas for houses has come into its own and it is both a serious business and great fun too.

I have not mentioned prices in the book. They are ever changing and, although on the increase, only prove that property must be one of the greatest investments there is. To give actual figures would be to date a publication which I feel should be timeless, cottage-life being something that is going to be (and indeed has been) in fashion for a long, long time. With the exception of a few luxury buys (and we all like to know about things we can't afford, but from which we can get inspiration), the costs of a large majority of the conversions were what were considered reasonable to people in the middle-income bracket at the time they were carried out; and the same applies to the price range of any new property described.

This is a book for the young, buying property for the first time with limited money to spend, showing what can be done with the most unlikely building, whether they do it for themselves or with the help of experts; for the more mature buying property for the second or third time round (for holiday and later retirement, perhaps) with a little more cash to buy those extra touches of comfort straight away; and for the man and woman who can afford a second home in Britain or Europe, somewhere a little bit different, where they can relax, far away from the frustrations of a busy career-life.

In fact, it is a book for everyone with a love of property, whether it is a cottage or barn, farmhouse or apartment. And it is not only intended for British readers. Home and abroad are only relative terms and can be anywhere to anyone. Other European nations are becoming equally conscious of the attractions of cottage living and the preservation of their heritage; and with Britain now a member of the Common Market, there could well be as many French cottage-seekers in Wales and the Lake District as there are British in the Dordogne district of France. The majority of Americans, too, are attracted to the old, traditional way of life in Europe, as well as being active in conserving what is best in their own culture and background.

Even if you are not considering buying any more property, you can always collect ideas from others to improve what you already have. "Collecting" property – mine and other people's – is now obviously my lifetime interest. I want to see them all, whether they are old chapels in Corfu, crofters' cottages in the Scottish Highlands, country houses in Cork or log-cabins in the USA – and write books on them too.

For ease of identity all picture references have their numbers in the margin adjacent to their relevant mention in the copy. In the case of colour pictures, the reference appears as a Roman numeral, printed in brown, together with the page number.

1 (above right)
Cottage living: Figures and Horses Outside a Suffolk Cottage painted by Edward Robert Smythe.
Oscar and Peter Johnson, Lowndes Lodge Gallery

2 (right)
Cottage living: The Cottage Door painted by George Morland, c. 1790.

7

3
*A sturdy stone cottage in the heart of the Welsh mountains.
(Welsh Cottage Property Advertiser, Aberystwyth)*

4
The American cottage: an early example of a weatherboarded house in Ohio, USA.

5 (below)
American Country Life in the grand style, 1855. October Afternoon lithograph by Currier and Ives from a painting by F. F. Palmer. John S. Rumbold Collection American Lithographs at Bearnes Salerooms, Bearnes and Waycotts, Torquay.

AMERICAN COUNTRY LIFE.

1
what is a cottage?

I will not change a cottage in possession for a kingdom in reversion.

Old Proverb

A cottage is a state of mind, a romantic image of worthwhile living, wherever it is.

Whether you use it for a weekend retreat, retirement or travel regularly to and from it while earning your daily crust, a cottage is a way of life. It does not have to be truly rural either, a cottage is a cottage in cities and towns too. If it is one of the ancient variety, it probably was on its own when it was first built and other dwellings grew up around it over the years.

It does not matter if it is large or small, a cottage can come in all shapes and sizes – its ambience spreads over chalets, farmhouses and barns. The down-to-earth dictionary definition of a cottage is, in fact, a small house! And down-to-earth is what you need to be, remembering a cottage is for living in. Big or small, ancient or modern, it does not really matter, you can stamp your personality equally well on contemporary bricks and mortar.

So before you set off on the problem-paved road to conversion, you must decide what sort of cottage is for you, whether you want one which needs full-scale restoration and renovation, or one that is virtually livable-in as soon as you step over the threshold.

Forget the estate agent's standard jargon, appetising though it may be, of mellow bricks, a wealth of old beams, inglenook fireplaces and other equally beguiling phrases. The important question is: is it what you want?

If, like me, you have a passion for property, however sad, dilapidated and undesirable it looks on first inspection, then you will have no difficulty in knowing almost at first sight whether a particular place is for you. Water may be dripping through the roof, your foot could catch in a rotten floor-board (wet rot) and fungus flourish furtively in a cupboard (dry rot), but you will hear the cry from its innermost depth: "Save me!"

Sometimes the cry comes too late and demolition is the only answer. I once had in my files an estate agent's "before" photograph of what was described as "a little gem ripe for conversion". Knowing that the place had been sold a year or so previously, I tramped the countryside in pouring rain, knee-deep in mud, looking for the "after" version. When I produced the photograph in the village I was told: "You wouldn't recognise it now". I was redirected to the grand house I had already seen in a clearing, and realised the little cottage was no more. Its general bad state of dilapidation, together with extensive damage caused by water from a spring under the floor, made salvation impossible. 13

"It didn't seem to worry the old boy who lived in it, mind you," the locals told me, but even they realised that the end had to come sometime, both for the occupant and his home.

Cherrytree Cottage was the one that got away – there are plenty of others which have been reprieved for a new long lease of life. 14

For instance, Rose Cottage, Coalbrookdale, 15, 16, 17 Telford, Shropshire, built about 1642, was nearly derelict, with the roof just about ready to fall in. It has been rescued by the Ironbridge Gorge Museum Trust Ltd., who are restoring it, using as much of the original material as they can, and recreating the old smithy and forge, which as Neil Cossons, the museum director told me, may well have been on the premises when it was originally built.

There are many Welsh hill cottages and farm cottages in France which have been lying derelict and abandoned for years, but they were built of such strong materials, such as granite and stone, that they have endured, if only as shells. Only recently has an actual cottage industry sprung up, 18 and the hunt is on to find somewhere old and 19 unusual, however much of a ruin, and bring it 20 back to life. Isolation is no deterrent, it is just 21 what today's "get-away-from-it-all" people 22 want.

This means cottages have become big business everywhere, which has naturally affected prices. Gone are the days when you could buy property for the proverbial song. However, the whole thing could come under the heading of progress, because the fashion for conversion has ensured the survival of many cottages and other buildings that would otherwise have been demolished by the ravages of time.

6 (above)
*Truly rural: an eighteenth-century needlework picture
conjurs up the simple, rustic life.
(Millar and Harris)*

7 (below)
*Cottage ambience in a suburb: Old Wyldes in Hampstead
Garden Suburb is a seventeenth-century, weatherboarded
farmhouse. Rare in Greater London, it is reminiscent of the
timber-framed houses of New England, USA. The painter,
John Linnell, lived in part of the house from 1823–27, and
visitors included George Morland and Constable.
(Greater London Council)*

8 (right)
Sad, dilapidated and undesirable: can this Welsh hill
cottage be saved?
(Trevor Kenyon)

9 (below)
The type of problem that has to be overcome in the restoration
of old property: renewing rotten timbers in the sub-floor. The
Surveyor's Guide to Timber Decay – Diagnosis and
Treatment. Stanley A. Richardson.
(Richardson and Starling)

11

10 (right)
True dry rot: merulius lacrymans, *showing the formation of globules of water or tears, from which the name* lacrymans *is derived.*
(Richardson and Starling)

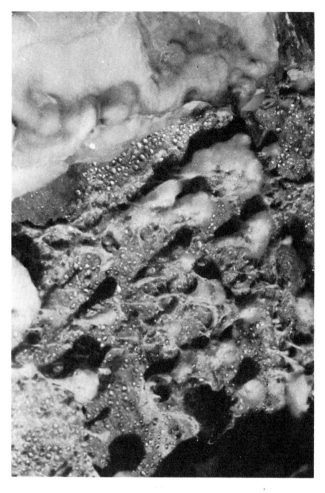

11 (below)
Wet rot: coniophora cerebella, *known as cellar fungus. The Surveyor's Guide to Timber Decay – Diagnosis and Treatment. Stanley A. Richardson.*
(Richardson and Starling)

12

12 (above)
The one that got away: Cherrytree Cottage, near Midhurst, Sussex. A spring underneath this cottage made demolition the only answer.

13 (below)
The one that took its place: much grander in style than its tiny predecessor it stands in beautiful National Trust land.

14 (left)
Saved: Skitreadons in Haslemere, Surrey, a fourteenth-century, picture-book cottage complete with exposed beams and inglenook fireplace is so called because the land on which it is built was believed to have once belonged to a man called Skit. Skitreadons originally meant Skit's clearing.
(Colin G. Futcher)

15, 16, 17
Rose Cottage, Coalbrookdale, Telford, Shropshire is believed to be one of the oldest cottages in the area. Although dated 1642, the timber framing indicates that it could be earlier. It was bought by The Ironbridge Gorge Museum Trust for restoration and conservation, and their first two jobs were to strip and repair the roofs of the second and third bays, below and top right. "The whole place was leaning very badly and the original truss beams had slipped," explained Neil Cossons, director of The Ironbridge Gorge Museum Trust Ltd. Most of the restoration work is being done with as much original material as possible, below right, and a blacksmith and forge will be built in the north end where they may well have been originally.
(The Ironbridge Gorge Museum Trust Ltd.)
(Trevor Kenyon)

I (right)
A cottage is a small house: The Wedge in Surrey, complete
with brilliant white outside walls, powder-blue window
frames and matching sweetheart shutters.
(ICI)

18
Conversion is underway to this cottage in Worthing, Sussex.
It has been completely gutted inside, given a new roof, and
new windows have been fitted.
(Trevor Kenyon)

19 (below)
Transformation: this simple brick cottage in a terrace in
Worthing, Sussex has been given a complete face-lift with
white-painted doors and shutters, and window-boxes. The
window on the top floor was blocked in during the time of the
window-tax.

II
The epitome of peace and quiet, charm and romance: a
thatched cottage set in a beautiful garden.
(Crown Paints and Wallcoverings)

20 (above)
The Brewers Cottage in Denbighshire, set in bluebell woods, is just ripe for reclamation. Built of stone and slate, it was originally used as a brewer's cottage on the Pennant Hall Estate. (Lightfoot and Newman)

21 (left)
This old farm cottage in the Dordogne district of France is just waiting to be brought back to life.
(Trevor Kenyon)

22 (below)
Away from it all: Pokabaig, an original crofter's cottage on Skye in Scotland, is about 200 years old, with an earth floor and slate and corrugated iron roof. The simple character of the cottage has been kept as much as possible in the restoration. (ICI)

2
cottages come in all sorts

If I ever become a rich man
Or if ever I grow to be old
I will build a house with deep thatch
To shelter me from the cold.

The South Country, HILAIRE BELLOC

There are so many different types of cottages – ones with thatched roofs, half-timbered cottages, cottages built of stone and brick – the permutations are endless.

II, III
page 18
page 35

23, 24, 25
26, 27, 28

Thatched cottages conjure up the epitome of romance, their "hat" of thatch transforming the dullest dwelling, whether it is covered in long straw (average life 10–20 years), combed wheat-reed (20–40 years) or Norfolk reed (50–60 years).

These figures are from the Rural Industries Bureau who point out that length of life is dependent on many factors – the quality of crop and materials, weather conditions, the situation of the cottage with regard to prevailing winds and trees and, of considerable importance, whether or not a skilled thatcher has done the job.

29

Cromwell Cottage in Berkshire, so called because some of the Protector's troops were once said to have been billeted there, was formerly four farmworkers' cottages built about 1630.

With its fair share of woodworm, damp and dry rot, ("What do you expect of seventeenth-century dwellings?" asked its owner, undaunted), it is now joined together as one, a picture-book, timber-framed, thatched cottage with seven rooms set out in single file on two storeys. Every room seems to be on a different level, but the sensitive conversion that has been carried out has the original beams exposed to give a feeling of spaciousness and continuity.

The cottage is kept warm by an oil central-heating system run with small, neat radiators which tuck in under cross beams along the walls. The fuel storage tank is hidden away at the back of the cottage and, as the cottage is some distance from the road, there is a filling point near the entrance, with underground pipes leading to the tank.

30

Shaston Way, a 400-year-old, thatched cottage stands on the site of the old road to Shaftesbury and it is from Shaftesbury's old name,

Shaston, that the cottage derives its name.

The problem here was damp walls and floors. The solution was a damp barrier kit to prevent the damp coming through the walls and pitch-epoxy coating was applied to the floors to seal them against rising damp.

Freefolk Cottage, Bletchley, Buckinghamshire, built about 1650, originally had two bedrooms and two small downstairs rooms. When it was modernised, a large kitchen, bathroom and lavatory were added, the staircase was moved and the two downstairs rooms made into one. Additional leaded windows were put in to let in more light.

The original charm and character of the thatched cottage remain. In almost every room some of the original timbers are still visible and at the front of the cottage in particular, the windows are original.

Heating is by natural gas, using a gas fire/back boiler unit which fits snugly into the chimney breast. It heats seven radiators and a towel rail, as well as providing a cosy gas fire in the hearth. Old-style radiators were replaced by up-to-date, slim-line ones which blend in unobtrusively with the décor.

Meadow Cottage, Bedfordshire, was what the architect, Victor Farrar, calls a "drift" cottage, half-timbered with a derelict thatched roof and approximately 25 feet by 13 feet (7·6 metres by 3·9 metres) on ground plan, consisting of two floors. A kitchen had been added which was breaking away from the main structure, and there were also a number of derelict sheds.

Because of its open position the property had to be enlarged very carefully. Not only was it important to preserve the original property as far as possible, it was necessary to raise the height of the new section to conform with building regulations. The problems of height were overcome by using Norfolk reed thatch – more practical in this case than other harder materials such as slate or tile and with a flowing line which gives continuity to the design.

Other problems arose, such as the necessity of underpinning the old structure. This had to be done in very small sections but, as the timbering to the original basic frame was in very good condition, the work was not as difficult as had been at first expected.

The result reflects the careful co-operation between the building team and the owners. The work took less than six months from start to moving in, by which time there were only minor works to complete.

True cottage-dwellers often have to be do-it-yourself enthusiasts too. Ashley Larmuth, a consulting engineer, and his late wife, a lecturer on historical and architectural subjects, did an enormous amount of the conversion work themselves on their various projects. Three of their conversions are featured in this book: Farm Cottage, Pym Gate House, and Merrythought Cottage.

Merrythought was a ruin of a place in Hertfordshire, with the roof stove in and no doors or windows intact. They bought it from a builder and it was in such a bad state he did not charge them for the cottage, only the site value and the profit he would have made building a bungalow on it.

"There was no water, gas, electricity, sanitation or even access!" recalls Mr. Larmuth. "It was damp, smelly, had water running down the walls, ceilings less than 7 feet (2·1 metres) high, and rats, bats, cats and dogs had the run of the place!"

The building was out of true, having slewed sideways at one end because years ago somebody had cut through two of the transverse beams to make a doorway. There were holes in the thatch, and the place was a sorry sight.

Mr. Larmuth told me about the rehabilitation saga which took four to five years in easy stages. "We engaged a builder to dig drains and connect water from the mains, and to dig out the floors and replace them with 5 inches (12·7 cm) of waterproof concrete. He promised to do this at once while we went on holiday. When we returned he had dug a 6-foot (1·8 metres) deep trench from the house to the boundary which made access almost impossible, so we had to hire a caravan to live in temporarily.

"Then my wife and I decided to go to work on the cottage ourselves, with the help of two building apprentices in the evenings and at weekends. They were most co-operative and reliable."

Restoration meant a good deal of cleaning of timbers and spraying them with wood preservative. Concrete blocks were used where the old wattle-and-daub infilling was failing, and timber posts which were hollow at the base were cut back and underpinned with brickwork or reinforced concrete. Two brickwork buttresses and a new supporting post stabilise the slewed-over end of the building. To gain headroom the floors at ground level are on average 9 inches (23 cm) lower than formerly, while bedroom ceilings have been raised. Over the centre of the principal bedroom the ceiling height was increased to 8 feet (2·4 metres) from 6 feet 3 inches (1·9 metres), leaving two interesting old cross beams exposed well below it. Finally the walls were re-rendered externally over an expanded metal mesh.

37

Mr. Larmuth did some of his own electrical wiring and plumbing, made windows, laid a new bedroom floor, built cupboards and did various carpentry jobs. He also built a porch for the new main entrance at the side, incorporating two windows taken from the front of the cottage. His wife acted as plumber's mate, did some plastering, laid floor tiles, and did all the interior decorating.

38

As it was once two cottages, the building naturally had, and still has, two staircases. One leads from the dining area of the living-room to a guest room only. The other, in order to gain space and improve communication between rooms, was taken out and replaced by a new winding stairway made in Parana pine by a local craftsman. No two steps in the flight are alike in size and shape.

39

To improve the light in the cottage, bay windows to east and south were built, and an extension at the rear – formerly the dairy and now used for wine-making – was re-roofed, using 250-year-old pantiles from the pigsties.

Have you ever seen a cottage that looks like three honey jars with cone-like hats of thatch on the top? I never had until I saw Honeypot Cottage by the River Thames in Staines, Middlesex. It is the home of actress/comedienne Beryl Reid, who describes her somewhat novel abode as having "a round bedroom, a round kitchen, a round dressing-room and a living-room sort of made up of the ends of the circles, if you see what I mean".

IV
page 35

40

She knew it was her dream cottage at first sight. "I fell in love with the place straight away. The people living there hated it," she said. "It had wet rot in the kitchen, and dry rot in the bedroom but I couldn't have cared less. As I looked at one disaster after another all I could say was: 'Ooh, marvellous!'"

41 The Wedge in Surrey, so called because it stands on a wedge-shaped piece of land between two other cottages, is a real example of how a little Cinderella of a dwelling can become a fairy princess. Bettie Spurling, television personality and public relations expert, transformed an ordinary, box-shaped cottage into a delightful place of character and charm.

There were few structural alterations to make, and most of the transformation has been done with small decorative touches and plenty of paint. "Sweetheart" shutters (plain strips of wood with a heart-shaped hole near the top) were added to make unimportant windows look larger and give them a bit of style and co-ordination. The original, simple, cottage front door was painted blue to match and given brass door furniture.

The whole of the outside brickwork was painted brilliant white, and the wrought-iron trimmed porch and cottage name plate, black. A novel touch in the concrete, crazy-paved terrace is the incorporation of friends' footprints.

Flowers and shrubs are everywhere – in old, white or blue painted barrels and in an unusual and most effective container made from a doll's cradle fixed to a stand.

Farm Cottage, Dorset, built of stone with a stone slab roof, was condemned as unfit for human habitation when Ashley Larmuth and his wife bought it. The ceiling on the ground floor was less than 7 feet (2·1 metres) high, the floors had rising damp, and water was oozing between the stone flags. There was no sanitation or water, the front wall was cracked from roof to foundations, bulging out for a length of about 8 feet (2·4 metres), and there was woodworm in the roof timbers.

The floors were excavated and replaced with waterproof concrete with lino tiles over the top. The offending bulge was dealt with by having the wall rebuilt from top to toe, and a bathroom and new entrance hall and front door were built on.

Electricity and water were installed, and an appropriate septic tank drainage system added.

23 (below)
Popples in Brettenham, Suffolk, with its numerous tiny windows and little footbridge over the stream to the door, has a superb example of a long straw, thatched roof. The timber frame is original.
(Council for Small Industries in Rural Areas)

24, 25 (right)
Examples of two different kinds of thatching: above, the thatcher works with long straw, and below, a scalloped thatch "apron" of combed wheat-reed decorates a cottage dormer window.
(Council for Small Industries in Rural Areas)

26 (above left)
Petoc in Tigley, Devon, a long, low, seventeenth-century
cottage, has a combed wheat-reed roof.
(Council for Small Industries in Rural Areas)

27 (left)
Oak Apples in Suffolk also has a combed wheat-reed roof but
with added diamond-pattern decoration along the ridge.
(Council for Small Industries in Rural Areas)

28 (above)
Holly Tree Cottage in Suffolk is thatched with Norfolk reed.
(Council for Small Industries in Rural Areas)

29 (above right)
Cromwell Cottage in Berkshire, built about 1630, was so
called because some of the Protector's troops were said to have
been billeted there. Originally four farmworkers' cottages, it
has been converted into one but still retains its original character.
(Maidenhead Advertiser)

30 (right)
Shaston Way, a 400-year-old thatched cottage in Wiltshire,
had damp walls and floors which were treated with Aquaseal
products. Note the unusual "patchwork" brick effect of the
side wall, and the original well in the garden.
(Berry Wiggins/David Robson)

31, 32
Freefolk Cottage in Bletchley, Buckinghamshire, above, built about 1650, was recently modernised by the Daniels, the present owners. In its conversion the two downstairs rooms have been made into one, left. The old fireplace remains and the room has been decorated in simple, country-style.
(The Gas Council/Focus 4)

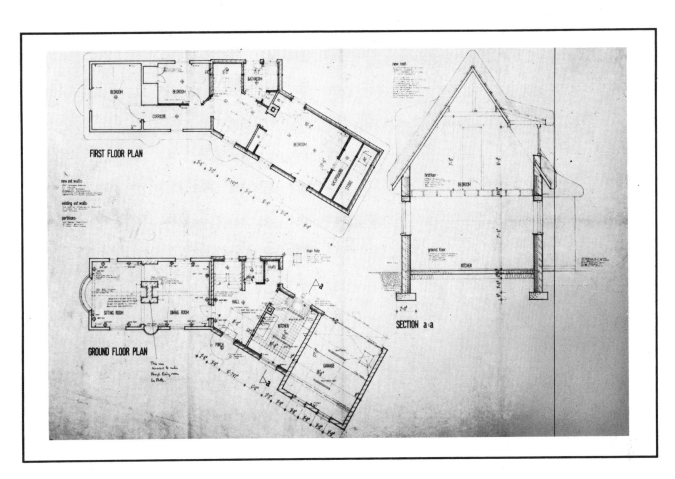

33
The plan of Meadow Cottage in Bedfordshire, showing the work that was to be carried out. This included new extension walls, a bay window, the removal of a fireplace wall to make a through living-room on the ground floor, and a new roof.

34, 35
Meadow Cottage, newly converted, above right, with a Norfolk reed thatched roof and the exterior painted white. The well in the garden is original. The dividing wall downstairs was removed to make one large through living-room with a bay window at the far end, right, and the original old cottage beams were exposed and cleaned.
(Commercial and Industrial Photographs)

36 (above)
Merrythought Cottage in Thriplow, Royston Hertfordshire before its conversion was two cottages. It was out of true and looked a sorry sight with holes in the thatch.
(Ashley Larmuth)

37 (below)
Completion of the conversion took almost five years – now the two cottages are one, the exterior has been re-rendered, the thatch renewed and new windows have been fitted.
(Ashley Larmuth)

38, 39
Merrythought Cottage interior before and after: the timbers on the stairway were rotten, above. The original straight flight led to a small landing which was once used as a space to sleep in. Right: the sitting-room and dining area after conversion. The cross beam on the left of the picture shows how the original structure had sagged, so the brick pier was added to give fresh support.
(Ashley Larmuth)

40 (above)
The living-room of Honeypot Cottage, the home of
actress/comedienne Beryl Reid on the River Thames at
Staines, Middlesex.

41 (right)
The Wedge in Windlesham, Surrey is so called because of the
wedge-shaped piece of land on which it stands between two
other cottages. Originally a simple, box-shaped cottage, it has
been transformed into a place of great charm, with
whitewashed walls, a blue door with matching sweetheart
shutters, and flower barrels.
(ICI)

42 (left)
Farm Cottage in Dorset before: this 300-year-old cottage was condemned. It had water rising through the stone-flagged floor, the front wall was cracked from roof to foundations and the timbers were rotting with woodworm.
(Ashley Larmuth)

43 (below)
The plan for renovation of Farm Cottage.
(Ashley Larmuth)

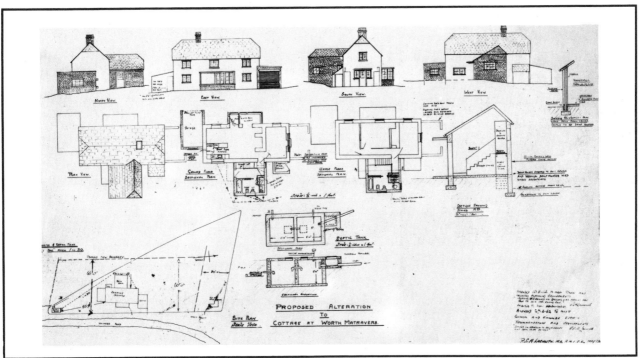

44 (left)
Farm Cottage after: complete restoration was carried out. The front wall was rebuilt, a new, large bay window was put in and a stone garage added at the side.
(Ashley Larmuth)

31

3
desirable regency residences

Not so much a conversion, more a way of life.

AUTHOR

Our cottage-style, terrace house on the south coast of England was referred to in estate agents' language as "a desirable Regency residence, overlooking sea and public gardens".

45

Desirable it appeared at first glance, being one of a terrace built evidently in the early nineteenth century; subsequent investigation, however, revealed it to be probably older than Regency. In one of the other houses in the terrace a piece of wood used for a mantelpiece was discovered during restoration bearing the words "Mantelboard J. Plaistow 1803". My husband and I fell in love with the place at first sight, panelled front door, odd windows, crooked balcony and all, and planned exactly where the piano would go in the sloping-ceilinged front room, and marked a spot by the balcony window for my desk.

Then came the icy douche of the surveyor's report. In precise, economical phrases, it referred to nail sickness, dead plaster, flaky paintwork, rot, attacks by woodworm and wood-boring beetle, sagging in the ceilings, drains that often brought water up instead of down, and a brief but to-the-point comment that there were occasions when the sea had been known to flow down the road and flood the basements of these desirable Regency residences!

Did this put us off? I am afraid not. If a cottage is a state of mind, what has realism got to do with it? It just became a challenge to put it right.

46

We decided to do the decorating and minor repairs ourselves, calling in the experts for wiring, plumbing and any large structural work.

V
page 36

The balcony had to be replaced; so did the sloping ceiling in the sitting-room – it fell down as soon as we took possession. Mind you, the ceiling did not look a great deal better when it was put back, fresh plasterboard nailed to the existing bowed joists. We cured that by taking the hessian paper used to decorate the walls over the ceiling. Bumps and irregularities disappeared like magic, merging with, and disguised by, the weave of the hessian, with the undulating join between walls and ceiling hardly noticeable.

What did we do with crumbling walls long hidden under layers of wallpaper in the hall and passages? Only the really bad parts of the walls were stripped to the bare lath and plaster (mainly lath, with little plaster left) and the moderately bad bits had the old paper stuck down again at the edges to hold in what lay beneath.

The top attic room scheduled to be the major bedroom was quite a problem. It was not in such bad condition, but the ceiling sagged badly in the middle, having broken away from the rafters above through nail sickness. The solution here was the relatively simple one of jacking up the bulge and strengthening the supporting rafters. The process was extremely successful, giving us an extra foot of headroom.

The kitchen was antediluvian and was in the basement which we did not want to use for the moment. But on the first-floor landing was a narrow, greenhouse-type room which at some time or other had been added on to the back of the house. It contained an old, cracked, porcelain sink, a gas point and virtually nothing else except a magnificent view of the sea and gardens at the window end, largely hidden by shelves full of flower pots.

On one wall we put a stainless steel sink unit and a gas cooker, and between the two an electric refrigerator with a working top. There was simply no other order in which to fit these essentials, and by the time the rubbish bucket had gone under the sink unit there was no room to store anything else on that side of the room.

Standard cupboards were no use at all, so some shallow fitments were made to run all the way along the opposite wall from floor to ceiling, combining open shelves, closed cupboards, and another working top surfaced with an old piece of marble found in a junk yard.

That was phase one of the restoration work. Phase two was several years later when we decided we could not wait any longer to have the leaking, conservatory-style roof in the kitchen lifted off and replaced with a solid one and new windows fitted. The work was extended to replace an unsafe wood floor with a concrete one, an operation which led to the discovery that the whole of the middle of the house appeared to be resting on one curved joist. The builder chalked on the joist the cryptic words "Please observe", without any further comment. There was no need.

Each house in the terrace, incidentally, is a little different from the other both inside and out, having been altered gradually over the years – quite fascinating, really. Scheduling by the authorities of local historic and architectural interest, with a preservation order on the frontages of the houses, came too late to preserve any real unity.

The backs of the houses have been altered and added to even more over the years than the fronts. Some have flat backs, others have a square, box-like wing of two or more floors added, with walls usually only one-brick thick, to provide more accommodation. Ours not only had the greenhouse-style extension on our little added box but a tile-hung protuberance suspended over the semi-basement area. This room was rather dark with a small sash window, so we replaced it with large French windows to open up and get the full impact of the view of the sea and gardens. Bars were put across the outside for security, so that there would be no danger of falling into the area below when the windows were opened wide.

What more fitting then, that phase three should be the addition of a balcony at the back of the house to walk out on and really appreciate the view? This was built and was a great success, making our Regency residence even more desirable.

The basement renovation was phase four and you can read all about it, together with its problems, in the next chapter. We forgot about phases after that – our cottage, house, call it what you will, had become not so much a conversion, more a way of life! One day I shall do a real research job on these desirable Regency residences, to find out more about them and trace their history from the time they were called "the buildings" on a local map of the early 1800s to the time they became what a recent observer called "a spot of Chelsea in West Sussex" – high praise indeed for the modest buildings.

45

Our desirable Regency residence in West Sussex as we first saw it – beginning to show its age. Subsequent investigation showed it to be probably older than Regency – c. 1800. (Trevor Kenyon)

46

The balcony was rotten and had to be replaced, together with the old "hangman" type supports. The cornice which was crumbling badly had to be levelled off, regrettably, as it was part of the unifying façade of the terrace. The whole of the exterior brickwork was painted with masonry paint, woodwork was painted black and the front door bright red. (Anthony E. Reynolds)

47 (above)
The back of our house after its alterations: French windows
were put in with bars across the outside for security. Next to it
is our box-like extension with its newly resurfaced walls, a
solid roof replacing the old glass roof, new windows and a new
concrete floor.
(Trevor Kenyon)

48 (right)
Each house in the terrace is a little different, having been
altered gradually over the years. Even with the differences,
though, the terrace presents an attractive appearance.
(Trevor Kenyon)

III (above)
Timber-framed cottage with a beautifully cut and patterned thatched roof.
(ICI)

IV (below)
Honeypot Cottage in Staines, Middlesex is the home of actress/comedienne Beryl Reid. At the bottom of her garden is the River Thames where she keeps a houseboat for her guests.
(TV Times)

V
The sitting-room of our Regency house in Sussex after conversion, with the original black, cast-iron fireplace. The walls are covered in hessian, the chairs in toning hessian-type fabric and the print over the mantelpiece, specially framed by John Campbell, London, is edged with pink silk. (Trevor Kenyon)

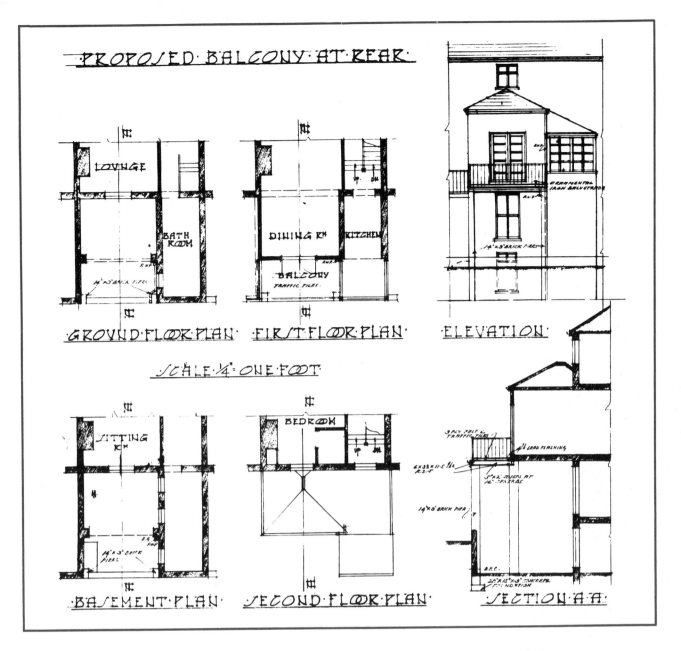

PROPOSED·BALCONY·AT·REAR·

LOUNGE

BATH ROOM

GROUND·FLOOR·PLAN·

DINING RM

KITCHEN

BALCONY
TRAFFIC TILES

FIRST·FLOOR·PLAN·

ELEVATION·

SCALE ¼" ONE FOOT

SITTING RM

BASEMENT·PLAN·

BEDROOM

SECOND·FLOOR·PLAN·

SECTION·A·A·

49 *(above)*
Our next step was to add a balcony at the rear of the house.
(Millar and Harris)

50, 51
The balcony is underway, the plan having been slightly
amended. Two new brick piers have been built to match the
existing two, right, and the first rolled steel joist has been
fitted to support the weight. We needed only to remove the
safety bars from in front of the French windows, below right,
and we could walk from our study/dining-room out on to
our new balcony overlooking the gardens and sea.
(Trevor Kenyon)

4
new life for an old basement

A comfortable house is a great source of happiness.
It ranks immediately after health and a good conscience.

SYDNEY SMITH

We were horrified by the problems that arose with our basement. There was damp, decay, rot and worm which meant that the work was both time-consuming and costly, though this was only to be expected in a house built around 1800 with no damp-proof course. Incidentally, after restoration, we called our basement the garden apartment which sounds so much more inviting; and after all it *does* back on to a garden.

The main thing that made conversion a little easier was that basically everything was there. Basements in these terraced houses were used as the main kitchen and this one had an old sink and an ancient dresser fitted on to the wall which had to go, as it did not survive its removal. In another part of the basement there was an old lavatory and bath.

The most telling way I can report the story of our garden apartment is to give a selection of the correspondence it evoked. It all started when out of the blue a letter came from the health department of the local council stating: "A survey of all the basement rooms in your area has recently been carried out by this department, and it has been found that the average height of the front basement room of your property is well below the 7 feet (2·1 metres) specified in Section 18(2)(a). Unless the height is increased the room is considered unfit by the provisions of the Housing Act.

"The normal procedure is to report this to the next meeting of the Health and Welfare Committee when it will be recommended that closing orders prohibiting the use of the unfit rooms for human habitation be made. Consent has been previously given that such rooms be used for domestic storage only.

"You will be notified when the Health Committee will formally discuss the making of a closing order and you or any person representing you may appear at this meeting and make any objections or proposals to the making of such an order as you may wish."

Surely it was not only the *height* of the room that made it unfit, we asked, and what did they want us to do about it?

Back came the reply: "The front room basement is unfit by reason of the following matters:
(a) Ceiling height less than 7 feet (2·1 metres). Average height at present 6 feet 6 inches (2 metres).
(b) Dampness.
(c) Insufficient natural light.
(d) Insufficient natural ventilation.

"Items (c) and (d) could be remedied by the provision of a new casement window frame, the whole of which could be opened to give increased ventilation, and of such design as to have a larger window glass area. In addition, the removal of the passage wall and the replacement of the existing wooden door with a glass door would give you a larger room with increased lighting.

"The remedying of (a) and (b) will be the most expensive items. This will involve the lowering of the basement floor 6 inches (15·2 cm) by excavation and the insertion of a waterproof membrane beneath the new main floor covering and up the sides of the walls."

We undertook to make the whole basement habitable. Actually, it was only the front room they were officially concerned about but we did not feel inclined to spend a large sum of money bringing one room only up to standard.

The council gave us six months to complete the work, but told us they would be understanding if it took longer. It was, in fact, some two years later that we received the accolade from the health inspector. "You have certainly made a good job of it," he told us.

Between those years a file full of letters flowed between us and the builder who did most of the work. The first one read: "We have pleasure in estimating for basement rooms and passage:

"Strip all ceilings and walls back to brickworks and joists. Strip off all fittings, cupboards etc. Lower floor by 6 inches (15·2 cm). Supply and lay 4 inches (10 cm) concrete to whole of oversite to new level of floor. Cut out chases for electrician. Treat the whole of the wall and floor surfaces two coats damp-proof membrane. Sand surface while wet to form key for plaster. Render and set the walls in plaster. Screed the whole floor area in sand and cement. Form concrete step at entrance approximately 12 inches (30·5 cm) high from outside ground level. Refit the existing doors, generally make good. Clear rubbish and leave site tidy on completion.

"Supply and fit new window to front elevation. Glaze, prime and paint on exterior only. Fit concrete lintel over opening in exterior wall.

"Please note: this estimate does not include interior decorations or electrical work."

It all sounded straightforward enough. We would do the redecorating using masses of white paint, and get the builder to arrange any electrical work necessary.

The estimate was for a few hundred pounds. The figure bore no resemblance to the final account which was about 10 times that amount. As work progressed, dormant damp, decay, rot and worm became apparent – years of neglect was being brought to light.

It all started to mount up when the old plaster was stripped away from the ceilings and revealed crumbling joists beneath. Left alone they might have gone on for years; disturbed, they had to be replaced immediately.

The builder summed up the whole question of the extras neatly: "I am concerned about the ground-floor joists. We have installed six new ones and if you look at these, you will observe that we will not be able to fit a level ceiling. Some of the remaining joists are in very bad shape.

"The extra works are beginning to accumulate and as it is not possible to give an estimate each time an extra item crops up, I suggest that this work be dealt with on a time and material basis."

The staircase which led into the main house was found to be worm-ridden and defective and had to be replaced by an open-tread version, the natural wood just being clear varnished to preserve the finish. This had to be specially tailored to fit, and the cost of making and the labour of fitting it was more again – another extra item.

Also extra was a window which had to be fitted into the inner wall between the two main rooms to take advantage of the natural light coming from the back window and the front. This was a much better solution than removing the passage wall as originally suggested, because the front door would then have opened directly into the front room.

The costs began to mount up, as well as the work. When you whip out the old bath to waterproof the wall behind, are you going to spend money putting old-fashioned equipment back? Replacements are inevitable. What happens to the old bath, the ancient cooker? You pay someone to take them away.

We were paying off some of the costs as we went along, (our bank manager must have thought we were renovating a palace, not a basement!) when the builder sent us a letter which can only be described as a masterpiece of understatement. It started: "I have been concerned regarding the cost of works to the basement which started off as a small job and have developed into a fairly large one with the additional work carried out.

"I have, therefore, prepared an interim account which, to say the least, is a bit of a shaker."

The details of the works carried out listed 28 items. Only the first referred to the original estimate – the other 27 were extras!

The "bit of a shaker" went like this:

1.   a. Works as per our estimate.
     b. Extra cost due to increased cost of labour and materials: 10%.

2.   a. Works to fitting window as per our estimate.
     b. Extra cost due to increased cost of labour and materials: 10%.

3. Shore-up as required and remove floor joists – renew where unsound. Remove defective hearths, remove trimmers and fit joists. Re-fix the existing flooring and provide new as required.

4. Fit battens to remaining old joists to level up ceilings – board, float and set in plaster.

5. Supply and fit corrugated lathing to walls, extra to work specified.

6. Remove the existing – supply and fit new staircase, made to fit existing opening width and height complete with hand-rail, assembled and fixed on site.

7. Supply and fit new door frames and doors – two inner, one front entrance – all complete with door furniture. Pack out frames to fix to irregular openings, make good and glaze.

8. Shore up floors of both rooms, cut opening through inner, one front entrance – all complete with door stops and glaze to form fixed light. Make good brickwork to reveal where suspect and unsound.

9. Pick out rotten and defective timber plates, remove glazed frame. Reinforce and rebuild part of wall between passage and front room. This wall almost collapsed when plaster stripped and frame removed. Rebuild pier end under rolled steel joist.

10. Renew defective rain-water pipe at front entrance.

11. Remove rotten door-frame to basement area, cast lintel over. Make good defective brickwork – cut off defective rendering to wall and render one grouting coat, one coat sand cement, one coat fine finish.

12. Remove the existing front door – cast in solid concrete threshold – fit water bar. Rabbet out bottom of door to fit water bar and re-hang and make good tile front entrance steps in quarry tiles – grout joints.

13. Make good hole where gas main enters through wall in waterproof cement to prevent water entering here.

14. Erect ladders to seal flues and supply and fit loose hood and wire over in $\frac{1}{2}$ inch (1·3 cm) wire mesh to disused chimneys.

15. Strip out existing water services. Supply and fit new copper services routed through ceiling joists, re-connect to basement and first and second floor services.

16. Clear customers own rubbish to tip. Tip fees.

17. Disconnect and remove gas services and pipework from basement.

18. Build up fireplace opening, form concrete slab over and make good. Rebuild defective brick piers as required.

19. Treat all new timber before fixing.

20. Fit trimmers to joist to stair-landing to make safe defective and unsafe floor.

21. Remove gas service on surface. Alter and re-route gas service running through basement through joists and connect to serve floors above.

22. Lag exposed water pipes on surface in front basement area.

23. Cut out defective sill to first-floor front window where water entering. Remove brickwork under. Cast in concrete under sill – supply and fit lead tray through wall and turn up under window. Hand cut and trim and fit extension to window-sill and make good frame. Make good brickwork and rendering and plaster internally and externally.

24. Supply and fit new architraves to rear window, doors and finishes.

25. Supply and fit cupboard around electrical meters in hall entrance.

26. Hire of lorry to clear extra rubbish accumulated from extra works. Tip fees.

27. Checking and testing drain from front basement area before surrounding in concrete and finally checking and testing on completion.

28. To labour not charged to any particular job number due to waiting time and alterations and additions of work by customer – and waiting confirmation and decisions on various points – stopping and restarting works.

It was a truly marvellous work schedule for anyone contemplating renovating a basement – and a small one at that. The builder did a brilliant job. Our garden apartment is now a most attractive place, complete with flower-filled back patio. Our friends love it. "It's so private, a little

world of its own," they say, when they have stayed there.

Just occasionally we send down a little prayer to Father Neptune to continue smiling on our "desirable Regency residence by the sea", to keep it bright, light and *dry*.

52
Converting the basement into a garden apartment was our next job. The basic equipment was there but the walls were in a sorry state, suffering from damp, decay, rot and worm. (Anthony E. Reynolds)

56
57
58

53
As work progressed, more and more problems came to light.
The walls had to be first covered with Newtonite corrugated
lathing to form a waterproof barrier.

55
The sitting-room in our garden apartment was at last complete. An extra window had been fitted into the inner wall to give more light, and we had painted the walls brilliant white.
(Anthony E. Reynolds)

56 (right)
The French windows behind the floral curtains in the dining area lead out to a flower-filled patio, and beyond the reeded glass door are the kitchen, lobby, bathroom and lavatory.
(Anthony E. Reynolds)

57
Red-tiled steps lead down to the entrance. The modern window on the left was fitted to replace the original sash window.
(Anthony E. Reynolds)

58 (left)
Entrance to the garden apartment is through a decorative, wrought-iron gate. The old flood wall has been retained.
(Anthony E. Reynolds)

5
grand old barns

A cold May and a windy
Makes a full barn and a findy (solid).

Old Proverb

"Early in the nineteenth century, when corn was at a high price at the end of the great war, great barns were reckoned to hold £1,000 worth of grain, to be threshed as required on the floors between the bays." This was written by Gertrude Jekyll, famous landscape gardener and architect (1843–1932), in her book Old West Surrey, published in 1904. As you can see, barns had to be well built to hold such valuable harvest.

She went on to lament: "The corn is now threshed in the field by steam machinery instead of being garnered and beaten out by hand, and the grand old barns no longer justify their existence."

The passing of the great barns for farming use put them on the market as strong, structurally-sound places to convert to dwellings. Some still retain their original flavour.

King's Barn in Berkshire was brought back to life by Irena Mardi, an architect who trained in Rome, and now practises in Britain. Because this great barn with its vast, thatched roof was scheduled as of historic interest, no dramatic changes were desirable to the outside of the building. Some windows obviously had to be put in and the problem was inserting them without spoiling the line of the weatherboarded walls. This was solved by putting small windows high under the eaves and grouping them informally so they did not interrupt the rhythm of the horizontal elm planking. On the garden side, larger windows could be fitted to give more light.

The interior retains that marvellous open-plan attraction of a barn. A gallery was built which covers only half the ground-floor area and provides space for three bedrooms, a study-area and a bathroom. The living and dining areas have the full height of the barn, planned round a central fireplace with the kitchen tucked neatly under the gallery.

Uniform floor tiling (blue paving bricks), is used throughout. Most of the original scarred and pitted rafters and beams have been retained, strengthened where necessary with steel columns and new timber joists.

Rudge Hall in Rudge, near Frome, Somerset is a magnificent Elizabethan barn of enormous charm and character, with a Cotswold tiled roof. The conversion to a house included an addition built in natural stone to blend with the original building; the original gabled dovecot was also restored.

The enterprising conversion was initiated by Viscountess Long of Wraxall through her country conversion company, Long Estates. On the ground floor the great galleried hall has exposed beams, stone fireplace and large stone mullioned windows. There are five bedrooms, two bathrooms, dining-room and kitchen, and central heating throughout.

For instant gracious living the conversion provided a small wine cellar stocked with wine and cigars. On the first floor is a minstrels' gallery with oak balustrading and a door through to a study or extra bedroom. Double French doors lead out on to a flat roof.

The Tithe Barn in Tredington, Warwickshire, is another great place built of stone with a Cotswold tiled roof and a black and white timber-framed, central gable. Skilfully remodelled with tile-hung dormer windows in the roof, and stone mullioned ones on the ground floor, it still retains its barn-like ancestry.

One of the features of the house is the garden room, 34 feet 8 inches by 12 feet 4 inches (10·5 metres by 3·7 metres). It has deep window seats overlooking the garden, exposed timbers on the ceiling and an angled fireplace with a large open hearth and stone surround, a portion of which is partitioned off with a built-in settle (a type of upright settee) and shelf. Open-tread stairs lead from this end of the room to the first-floor landing where an oak-galleried staircase leads to five bedrooms and two bathrooms.

Above the garage is a studio apartment, dominated by a main roof truss of the cruck beam. (Pairs of crucks, incidentally, were bent trees roughly shaped, joined together at the top, and opening out at the bottom and resting on stones; they were used to support the roof of early barns and houses.) The big living-room contains the kitchen too, with a breakfast-bar built on a natural stone base to act as a room divider, in keeping with the building.

71
The Barn, Collingham, in Nottinghamshire, (documents relating to it go back to before 1821), is the home of Geoffrey Bray and his wife. With the help of a local builder, W. A. J. Russell, and a local authority grant which covered part of the modernisation costs, they transformed a tumble-down building into a dream house in less than 12 months.

72

73
Grange Barn, Buckinghamshire, an eighteenth-century, stone-built barn, has been converted into a four-bedroomed, two bathroomed house with minstrels' gallery, exposed beams and a stone fireplace.

X, XI
page 71
Although The Barn in Sussex looked like a cottage, the deeds revealed it to have been a barn which was used as a granary in the mid-nineteenth century. It had also been used as an upholsterers' and furniture store too, and was filled with everything from bed-springs to broken-down Victorian chairs. On the face of it, it did not seem to need a drastic amount of doing up. It had the necessary amenities – a bath, toilet and kitchen – but they were rather old-fashioned and obviously needed replacing. The outside had rather a lot of ugly pipes up the front where the plumbing had been put in over the years, but there was not much that could be done about them without major alterations.

The building, constructed of Sussex blue-nosed flints, had sash windows, and double doors on the first floor where a window would normally have been. These doors had originally been used to take in sacks of grain, and the old hoist was still there.

The owners did much of the renovation them-selves. The inner walls had a lot of crumbling cement which was bound together with a strong plastic substance – a sort of mushroom soup mix which dries off white – and then painted over with brilliant white emulsion.

Once started, the work piled up, as it generally does once old property is disturbed. The owners had a nasty moment when a long crack was dis-covered on the main exposed side wall. It had to be hurriedly filled in from top to bottom with cement, and they were warned that if it got worse a tie-rod would have to be put in to prevent the wall bulging.

Another part of the wall had been so badly affected by weather that it had become very thin and had to be treated with a ready-mixed cement plastered over flat chicken wire to provide a key and added strength. When some "make-do"

repairs to the staircase were peeled off, it was found to be in a pretty dangerous condition, worm-eaten and insecure.

A local timber merchant made a knock-down replacement ready to put up, after being given the height and the number of steps required. They did the rest, prefabricating it in sizes to comply with building regulations which specify the correct height and width of tread.

The biggest problem was what to do with the old staircase after it was removed. Eventually it was cut in half to make it easier to handle. The two halves were put side by side and used as a shelf to store tins of paint on each tread, with cement and other heavy materials on the floor underneath.

The floors were crumbling and rotting in places, although the joists themselves were in good condition. New floors were made by laying $\frac{1}{2}$-inch (1·3 cm) chipboard in large panels over the old wooden floors.

The underside of the ceiling joists were visible and it was a case of either securing a ceiling to the beams or making the most of them as they were. This seemed much more appropriate but there was just as much work as in fixing a new ceiling. All the cracks in the planks above had to be filled in to prevent dust and grime from the floor above coming through, and the joists were then painted with black emulsion paint which goes on so much easier than gloss paint to cover blemishes and give a uniform appearance.

The accommodation plan is a large through X living-room downstairs which leads into a tiny kitchen where the old porcelain sink was replaced with modern units. Upstairs there is a big room which could have made two, but the owners felt it was much better, and lighter, to keep it as a large bedsitting-room.

At first it lacked a focal point, but the installa-tion of a fireplace between the two windows over-looking the garden remedied this. Unfortunately, the wall between was defaced by some rather ugly plumbing from an obsolete central-heating system. To save the cost of removing this and to make a virtue of necessity, a narrow, mock chimney-piece was built out in plasterboard, edged with random wood planks from the demolished staircase, and a black-painted hood was fixed above the open fireplace which housed an electric fire.

The roof was not in bad condition, but to avoid any risk of slates blowing off and letting in water, a water-proofing process was adopted, carried out by the Turnerised Roofing Com-pany. A hot, weather-proofing, black solution was applied all over the roof, followed by a covering of cotton cloth and a second application of the hot, black solution.

The Old Barn in Carperby, Wensleydale, is a project of Your Cottage in the Country Ltd., a company in York specialising in the conversion of unusual properties. Corporate members of Britain's National Trust organisation, they have a genuine concern for the preservation of old buildings, and some particularly ingenious ideas for their conversions.

This sturdy, stone-built barn near Castle Bolton where Mary Queen of Scots was so long interned, has external stone steps to the first floor. It has been imaginatively converted, with a minstrels' gallery above a dining-room, two bathrooms and the original stone staircase retained. A natural dry stone wall forms the boundary of a patio reached from the living-room by French windows, and upstairs there are both internal and external balconies.

The Old Barn in West Witton, Wensleydale, is a large, long barn overlooking the Yorkshire Dales. With no existing services, mains electricity, water and sewage services had to be brought in.

Ann McGeehan, company secretary of Your Cottage in the Country, the firm which organised the work, describes the clever conversion which produced a four-bedroomed, two-bathroomed house, with an apartment for elderly parent, teenager or au pair girl. "The dining/kitchen area now covers the space originally taken by the mistle, the old cattle stalls, and an external patio has been formed to take advantage of the sun from the south. There is an internal gallery or balcony running over the lounge, which looks from the ground floor straight through to the open beams above the second floor.

"This gallery forms a type of birdcage walk and connects the bedrooms to one staircase, although bedroom number two can also be reached by an external set of stone steps retained on the north face.

"A carport, built in local stone, provides an additional feature, and a garden store and tool store are incorporated in its construction. Wherever possible we prefer not to put doors on our garages, as these tend to be unattractive and to stop the circulation of the air, which dries and warms the motor vehicles. There is also a bedroom downstairs which could be used as a study if you wanted."

Starbotton Barn in the Yorkshire Dales, also a Your Cottage in the Country conversion, was in an idyllic setting, but the roof had collapsed, the place was full of worm, there were no sewers and its original appearance was not particularly impressive.

It has now been transformed into a most attractive house with three bedrooms and a bathroom on the ground floor, and the living-room and kitchen on the first floor to take advantage of the magnificent views. There was not much land with the property, but a garage was built with a good "turn-around" area.

59
King's Barn in Berkshire before conversion with no windows. Scheduled as of historic interest, no dramatic changes to the outside of the building were desirable.

47

60 (above)
The interior of **King's Barn** *before.*

61 (below)
The magnificent timber beams inside King's Barn.

62 (above)
King's Barn after its conversion: small, neat windows have been discreetly inserted high under the eaves so as not to interrupt the rythym of the horizontal elm planking.
(John Gay)

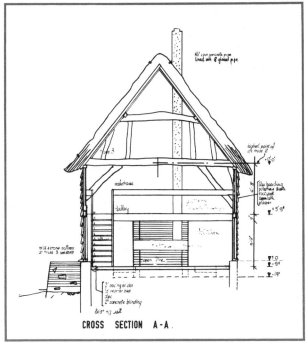

CROSS SECTION A-A.

63 (right)
The cross-section of King's Barn shows the arrangement of the gallery which covers only half the ground-floor area, and the central open fire with a cylindrical flue rising to the roof.

64

*The open-plan living-room, with the kitchen leading off, is
planned round a central fireplace and has the full height of
the barn. Above the kitchen runs the gallery which provides
space for three bedrooms, a study area and a bathroom.
(John Gay)*

65
Close-up of the study area in the gallery shows how well the curve of the old beam complements the new timber shelving and modern equipment.
(John Gay)

66 (right)
Rudge Hall near Frome in Somerset is an Elizabethan barn conversion with a Cotswold tiled roof, a new extension built in natural stone, and the original gabled dovecot restored.
(T. C. Leaman)

67
On the ground floor of Rudge Hall is the great galleried hall with magnificent exposed beams. Up the stairs from the hall is the minstrels' gallery with oak balustrading, off which is a study or extra bedroom.
(T. C. Leaman)

68, 69, 70
Tithe Barn in Tredington, Warwickshire, above, has been skilfully converted to retain some of its barn-like character, with its tile-hung dormer windows in the roof and stone mullions round the leaded light windows on the ground floor. One of the features of the house is the garden room, below left. It has exposed beams, an open fireplace and window seats which overlook the garden. Over the garage is the studio apartment, below, dominated by a main roof truss of the cruck beam. A breakfast bar, built in natural stone, divides the kitchen from the living-room.
(Edwin C. Peckham)

VI (above)
The top attic room of our Regency house was converted into
the main bedroom with the walls and fitted wardrobe
covered in textured wallcovering and the whitewood chest-of-
drawers unit painted white.
(Trevor Kenyon)

VII (right)
Our galley-style kitchen has Victorian tiles over the sink and
hatch doors into the dining-room. The opposite wall is fitted
with shelves and the windows overlook the garden and sea.
(Trevor Kenyon)

VIII (right)
The back of our house before: the box-like extension has walls
mainly one-brick thick, a glass roof, windows in poor
condition and a wood floor.
(Trevor Kenyon)

IX (below)
Rebuilding in process: an inner lining of breeze-blocks is
being fitted and a new window has been put in.
(Trevor Kenyon)

71, 72
*The Barn in Collingham, Nottinghamshire, c. 1821, before
and after the conversion, which took under 12 months.
(Focus 4)*

73 (above)
Grange Barn in Buckinghamshire, an eighteenth-century, stone-built barn, has been converted into a four-bedroomed house, with a minstrels' gallery, beams and a stone fireplace. (Richard Anderson)

74 (below)
The Barn in Sussex, once used as a granary in the mid-nineteenth century and later as a furniture store, has been transformed into a cottage of character. The picture shows the exterior before it was painted. (Trevor Kenyon)

75, 76
The plan for the new exterior of The Old Barn in Carperby, Wensleydale, right, shows changes to the existing windows and doors, a new balcony and, on the west elevation, existing out-buildings extended to form a garage. The plan of the interior, below right, shows dining, kitchen and living areas on the ground floor and bedrooms, bathroom and shower-room on the second floor.

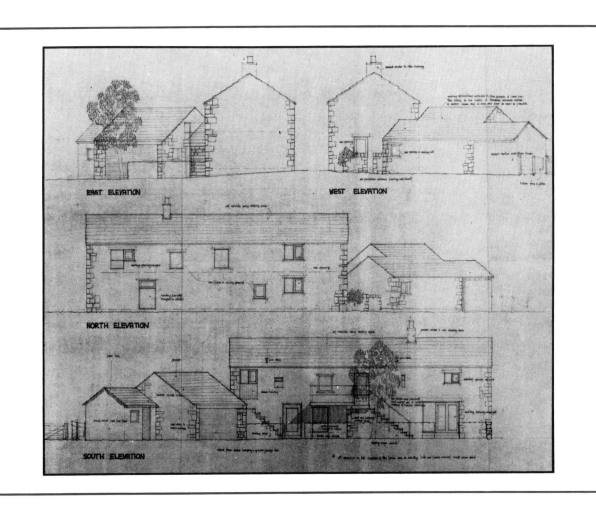

EAST ELEVATION

WEST ELEVATION

NORTH ELEVATION

SOUTH ELEVATION

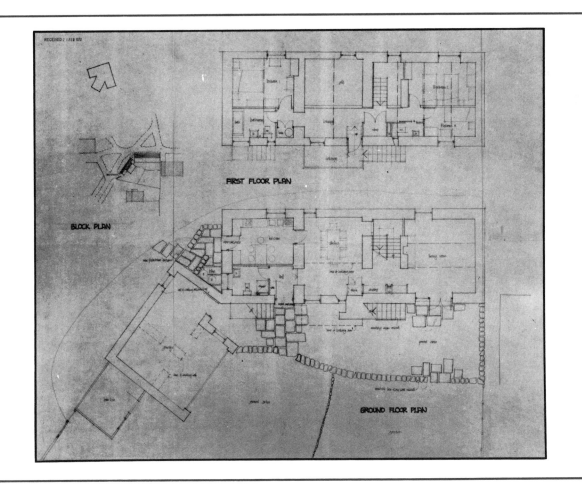

BLOCK PLAN

FIRST FLOOR PLAN

GROUND FLOOR PLAN

77 (left)
The Old Barn in West Witton, Wensleydale, a long barn built of local stone, overlooking the Yorkshire Dales, had no existing services when it was taken over for conversion. Mains electricity, water and sewage services had to be brought in. (John Gresswell)

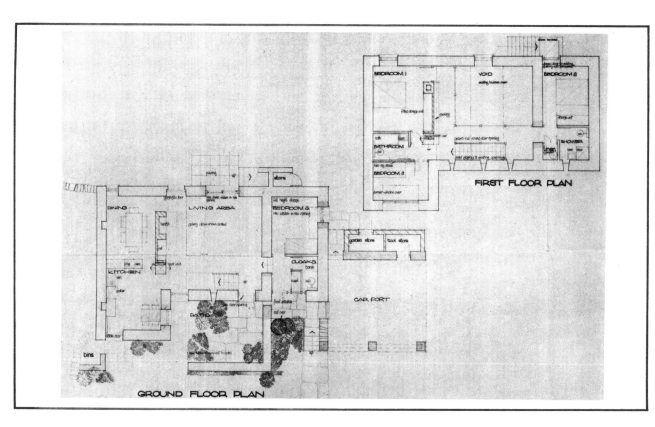

FIRST FLOOR PLAN

GROUND FLOOR PLAN

78, 79
The plan of the interior of The Old Barn, above, shows an extra bedroom on the ground floor. Upstairs, Bedroom 2, with large storage cupboards, shower, lavatory and basin, has its own stone staircase outside which means it can be used as a separate apartment for guests, elderly relatives or teenage children. The drawing, left, shows the interior of the barn with an internal gallery running over the lounge. (J. P. Little)

80 (above)
Starbotton Barn, in an idyllic setting in the Yorkshire Dales,
was in a terrible state of dilapidation. The roof had
collapsed and the whole place was full of worm.

81 (below)
The plan for conversion shows three bedrooms and a bathroom
on the ground floor, and the kitchen and living-room on the
first floor to take advantage of the magnificent views.

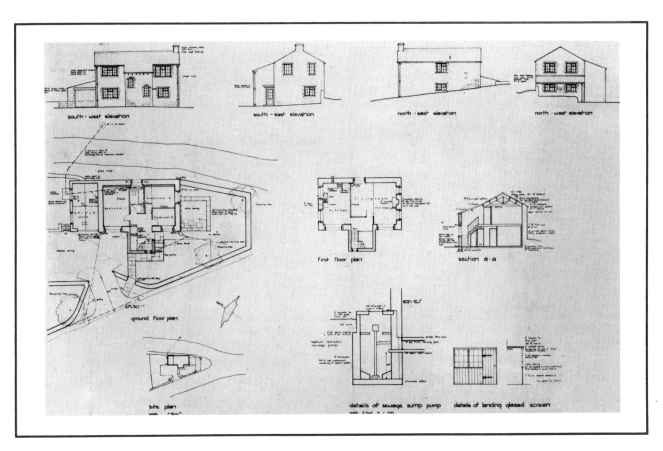

59

6
adding a room

Beauty crieth in an attic and no man regardeth.

A Psalm of Montreal, SAMUEL BUTLER

If you find yourself with not enough room because the family has grown so much, the obvious solution is to move. But by converting the house you already have – adding a room, raising the roof, adding a wing or just extending the kitchen – you could solve the problem more easily.

If you have a roomy attic, garret or loft you can convert it into another room. The idea is not new – servants used to sleep under the eaves during Elizabethan days. In some houses the wasted space in the loft can account for as much as 25 per cent of the total cubic capacity of the whole property.

"You can quite easily convert this wasted space into a useful extra room, however full of water tanks and pipes it is," says John Martin of Roomaloft Conversions, a company which specialises in raising the roof. "What is usually required is a new suspended floor so that no weight is transferred to the existing ceiling joists which are seldom strong enough to carry the additional load. A dormer window is needed to provide light and headroom together with new, purpose-made stairs for access and proper walls all round."

I found the most common kind of loft conversion is a simple, dormer-window extension which, with a ridge height of around 8 feet 6 inches (2·6 metres), is sufficient to allow a new ceiling height of 7 feet 6 inches (2·3 metres) over a fair proportion of the room. Where the ridge height is too low to take a new room, the old roof can be removed and a penthouse with a mansard roof made, that is, a roof constructed in two pitches.

Instead of facing the cheeks of the new dormer with weatherboard, the old tiles that were taken off the roof can be used to make the extension. It stops the dormer having that "stuck-on" look. The new dormer roof should have its own gutter and drain-pipe to drain away rainwater.

82 Two dormer windows and a rooflight window put into the roof of a house in London meant extra accommodation could be built to produce 83, 84, 85 a large studio and a child's bedroom. An open 86 plan staircase, with a spiral effect, was added to give access to the studio and bedroom.

Another conversion to a house in London produced a double bedroom and bathroom with shower, and a large lobby. 8 In keeping with the style of the original staircase, "single wind" stairs with risers and upright balustrade rails were fitted.

Floors are in 1-inch (2·5 cm) tongued and grooved boarding on softwood joists. The walls are in ½-inch (1·3 cm) foil backed plasterboard supported on timber studwork and were either wallpapered or plastered.

When Michael Brandt, who has his own company for the production of documentary and commercial films, wanted extra rooms for his cottage, he built on a whole wing.

The original was a system-built Colt timber house, which is prefabricated, section by section. First built in 1939 to the design of C. F. Colt, it was occupied by the Curator of the Colt Clavier Collection of Historical Keyboard Instruments before Michael Brandt bought and converted it.

The house had one large sitting-room and a small kitchen downstairs, with two small bedrooms and a bathroom upstairs. The alterations – current Colt houses use standard sections for extensions and enlargements – gave a new large kitchen and a dining-room downstairs (the existing kitchen became a utility room), and two more bedrooms and a second bathroom upstairs. An existing studio was moved to a site in the grounds to make room for the extension.

The step-by-step photographs of the work, taken by Michael himself, show that timber-frame means what it says – the house is built round a frame of wood, like the old Tudor houses. The timber frame carries the weight of the house, instead of walls of brick, block or stone. The result is a really worthwhile extension in keeping with the original dwelling.

No one ever has a large enough kitchen, so extending the area which is often the heart of the home is a top priority job. Careful planning is the secret when space is at a premium, and a specialist in the business is Roma Jay who runs Jay Kitchen Consultants. She can transform the smallest, dullest kitchen into an exciting place where the whole family will want to congregate.

In the Jays' first home the problem was too many doors (into hall, dining-room, larder and garden), unsightly pipes and haphazard storage. The larder door was taken away, and the useful space became part of the room into which trim modern cupboards were fitted – a tall slim one to take awkward cleaning utensils and top cupboards which fitted snugly over the refrigerator and new gas boiler.

The old cooker was replaced by a shiny, new, split-level version, with the oven fitted into the wall, and cupboards built underneath. The wide hob, with more cupboards underneath and a copper hood over, went on the old larder wall at right angles to the new twin sink, the two bowls more useful than a single unit and drainer. For eating, a long table, bar-style, swivels out from the main work surface. It seats four and also doubles as an ironing-board.

Roma Jay's next kitchen conversion was an even bigger challenge to her talents as a kitchen designer. Together, the kitchen and scullery possessed five doors, and the walk-in larder adjoined an outside lavatory. By blocking in the larder door in the scullery and moving the lavatory back into the space, she was able to extend the old lavatory area by 5 feet (1·5 metres) along the side of the house, to produce an integral utility room. Regulations insist on a ventilated lobby with two doors between the lavatory and kitchen, so this utility area was the perfect solution, as well as providing a home for the laundry equipment, brooms, and so on.

The next step was to demolish the wall dividing the scullery and kitchen to give a combined area of 14 feet 6 inches by 8 feet 6 inches (4·4 metres by 2·6 metres). The eating area was created by fitting a curved bench-seat around the L-shaped wall between the hall door and utility door, which was separated from the working part of the kitchen by a small peninsula unit.

The peninsula was carefully designed to contain a square sink and a half bowl, which holds the waste-disposal unit. The base unit opens on three sides, with a dishwasher in the corner facing the dining side. Dirty crockery is scraped and stacked into the machine straight from the table or trolley when entertaining in the dining-room. The worktop overhangs the back of the base unit and provides a bar for quick snacks. It also makes sitting down and working at the kitchen sink a practical proposition, as knees tuck under the bar with no effort. The advantages of using a sink from two positions are obvious.

Roma used this type of sink because the 12-place dishwasher she chose makes washing-up almost non-existent and a drainer unnecessary. Ideally a waste-disposal unit should have its own sink, but instead of taking up all the room needed for two bowls, a sink and a half seemed the best solution.

The sinks, hob and refrigerator are sited at right angles to each other and everything is within an arm's length. Even the corner base unit has been designed as a revolving cupboard to save unnecessary searching for contents.

All the ceiling-high wall cupboards and base units were specially made, and are in natural wood finish. The very necessary extractor fan is ducted through a dummy cupboard to an outside wall.

The larder, oven and 6 feet (1·8 metres) of base units and wall cupboards are on the opposite wall, while the rotisserie and grill sits above the hob on specially-made brackets.

Kiln Cottage in Kent is as picturesque as its name, but the kitchen was a problem. It was an awkward shape with so many doors and alcoves that it was impossible to have a useful run of work surfaces. The family wanted to be able to eat in the kitchen and have enough room for a separate laundry area. 97

Conversion was carried out in the following way: the room was split by an L-shaped peninsula unit with wall cupboards suspended above it which not only provided the much needed uninterrupted flow of working surfaces, but isolated the working part of the kitchen. A large larder was demolished to give way to a refrigerator and base unit, which were linked at right angles to the cooker and twin sinks. By siting the dishwasher next to the sink, facing outwards towards the eating area, this space was utilised to the best advantage. 98

A cosy eating-area was created on the other side of the kitchen in an alcove previously occupied by the boiler. This has now been replaced by a central-heating boiler positioned in a corner; a cupboard built above provides airing space.

Another alcove near the working part of the kitchen was converted into the laundry area, the space of about 5 feet (1·5 metres) being bridged by a work surface and a round sink which covers the washing-machine. Not only can hand-washing be done here, but all the plumbing for the sinks, dishwasher and washing-machine has been centralised, thus economising on services.

Another conversion that the Jays took on was the extension of a small kitchen to provide an eating area. This was achieved by dividing peninsula units with two-way cupboards above. The 99

100

hob and sink were installed on the long outside wall – easy for plumbing – with the oven at right angles. The cupboards reaching the ceiling were fitted for storing the sort of items that are only seldom used.

Another kitchen addition meant extending the room by 4 feet (1·2 metres) into the garden. This did not pose too much of a problem, but it still required careful planning to give the owner the utility area she wanted.

Created in the space previously occupied by a larder and walk-in pantry, the utility room houses not only the washing-machine and spin-dryer, but also a small, round sink and a broom cupboard. This left an area of 11 feet by 9 feet (3·3 by 2·7 metres) for the kitchen and, so that full use could be made of all four walls, the back door was moved from the kitchen to the utility area. There is now an uninterrupted run of white floor and wall units, and the muddy boots and other treasures the children bring in from the garden are safely deposited in the utility area, out of sight. A new hob and oven complete the new kitchen.

82
Raising the roof to provide extra accommodation: two dormer windows and a rooflight window were inserted into the tile-hung roof of a house in Hampstead, London.
(Millar and Harris)

62

83, 84
The extra space in the attic was needed for a large studio room, above, and a child's bedroom, right. The studio is light and airy with the dormer and rooflight window, and the space under the eaves has been used for cupboards. The shelving in the child's bedroom has been neatly fitted to dovetail into the sloping wall and the use of wallpaper helps to divide the sleeping area from the rest of the room. (Millar and Harris)

85, 86
Access to the studio room and child's bedroom is by an open-plan staircase winding spiral fashion at the top and bottom. The art-nouveau style wallpaper highlights the wall which shows through the open treads.
(Millar and Harris)

87, 88, 89, 90, 91
Installing a cedar-cheeked dormer window into the roof of a house in Finchley, London, meant the attic space could be converted into a double bedroom with adjoining bathroom and lobby. The bedroom has a wall of fitted wardrobes and the bathroom a built-in shower unit. Access to the new rooms is by "single wind" stairs with risers and upright balustrade rails, in keeping with the original staircase.
(Millar and Harris)

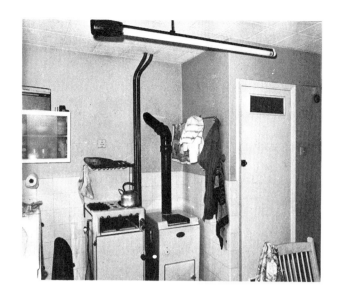

92, 93

Roma Jay's former kitchen before its conversion, above left, had far too many doors – into the hall, dining-room, larder and garden – unsightly pipes and haphazard storage. The larder door was taken away, above, and replaced by modern cupboards next to which stand the refrigerator, new gas boiler and new cooker hob with copper hood. The bar-type table tucks away under the main work surface when it is not being used for meals.

94a

This kitchen conversion was an even bigger challenge to Roma Jay's talents as a kitchen designer. The plan shows the kitchen before: 1. door to garden 2. boiler 3. dresser 4. refrigerator 5. door to larder 6. door to hall 7. side door 8. butler sink 9. cooker.

94b

Plan of the kitchen after: 1. food store 2. oven 3. base units 4. wall cupboards 5. one and a half sink and dishwasher 6. hob 7. eating area 8. new side entrance.

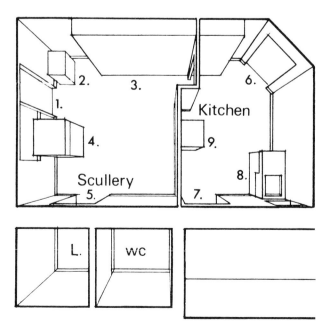
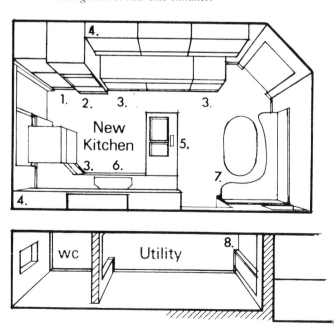

95, 96

The peninsula unit, right and below, contains a square sink and a half bowl which holds the waste-disposal unit. The base unit opens on three sides with a dishwasher in the corner, and the worktop overhangs this base unit to provide a bar for quick snacks. The eating area, below, is created by a curved bench seat with an oval table. Louvre doors lead into a lobby which contains more equipment, cupboards and a cloakroom. (John Maltby)

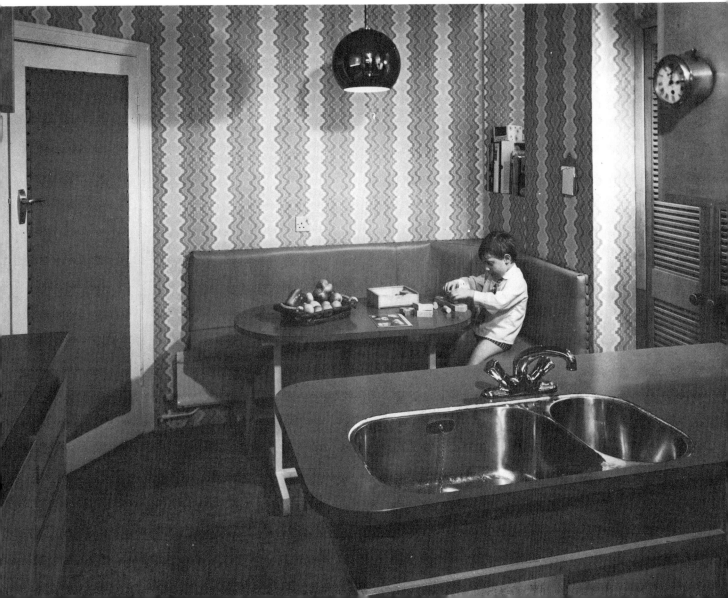

97

*The kitchen in Kiln Cottage was an awkward shape before
its conversion. It had so many doors and alcoves that it was
impossible to have a convenient run of work surfaces. The
family wanted an eating area in the kitchen and enough room
for a separate laundry area.*
(Jay Kitchen Consultants)

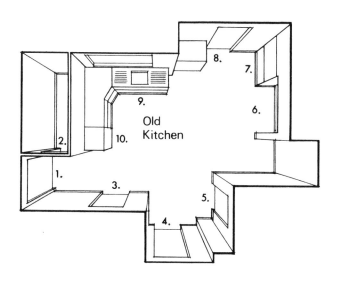

98a

*Plan of the kitchen before: 1. door to garden 2. larder
3. door to playroom 4. broom cupboard 5. door to hall
6. boiler in alcove 7. hatch 8. utility room 9. sink unit
10. cooker*

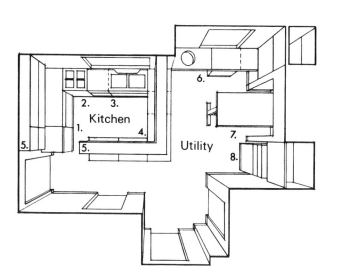

98b

*Plan of the kitchen after: 1. refrigerator and base units
replacing larder 2. cooker 3. twin sinks and dishwasher
4. base units 5. wall cupboards 6. washing machine and round
sink 7. eating alcove 8. boiler and cupboard above.*

99 (above)
The family wanted their long, narrow kitchen extended to
provide space for an eating area.
(John Maltby)

100 (below)
Peninsula units with two-way cupboards above were fitted
to make a room divider and provide an eating area.
(John Maltby)

101 (above)
The hob and sink were installed on the outside wall for easy plumbing, with the washing machine and oven at right angles. Ceiling-high cupboards open easily with a "lift-up" action and provide plenty of storage space for little-used items. (John Maltby)

X, XI, XII, XIII, XIV
The ground floor of The Barn in Sussex, top right, was filled with everything from bed-springs to broken-down Victorian chairs before its conversion, remnants of the days when it was used as an upholsterers' and furniture store. It was originally built for use as a granary in the mid-nineteenth century and on the first floor, top far right, the striped canvas covering headed "Max load 5cwt" conceals the door through which the sacks of grain were hoisted up. After conversion, centre right: a small kitchen has been added leading off the living-room and upstairs the large through room, centre far right, is used as a bedsitting-room. The exterior of The Barn, below right, was completely re-painted and the roof was treated with water-proofing substance. (Trevor Kenyon)

XV (far right)
The Old Barn in Carperby, Wensleydale was taken over for conversion by a company called Your Cottage in the Country. The existing openings in the barn were enlarged to accommodate large windows and two new ones were added.

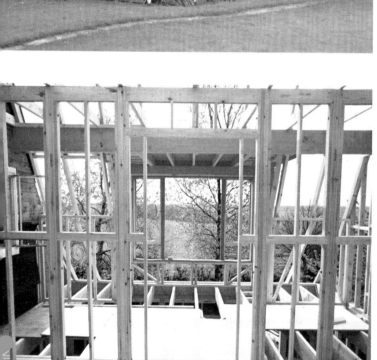

102a (right)
The owner of this kitchen wanted a utility room separated from the rest of the kitchen, so that muddy boots and other treasures the children bring in are safely deposited out of sight. This extra space meant extending the room into the garden. The plan shows the kitchen before: 1. larder 2. pantry 3. back door 4. door to breakfast room 5. sink unit 6. cooker.

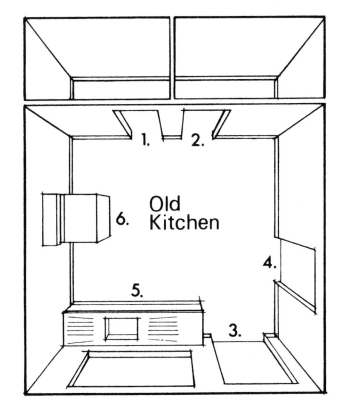

102b (right)
The plan shows the kitchen after, complete with new utility room: 1. 4-foot (1·2 metres) extension blocking back door 2. new back door 3. oven and larder 4. twin sink and dishwasher 5. hob 6. refrigerator 7. snack bar 8. base units 9. wall cupboards.

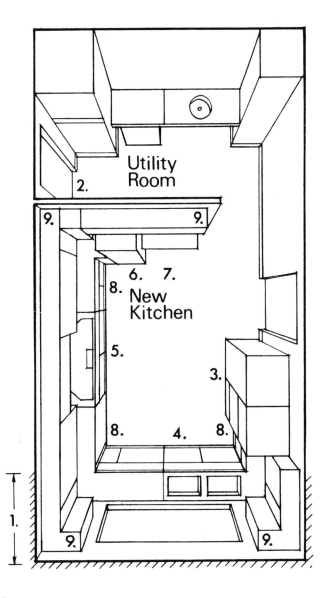

XVI, XVII, XVIII, XIX, XX, XXI
Michael Brandt wanted to add an extra wing to his system-built Colt timber house in Pluckley, Kent, top far left. The ground-floor timbers were constructed first, top left, to house a new large kitchen and dining-room, then the first-floor frame was added, centre far left and centre left, to provide space for two more bedrooms. The interior of the new wing, below far left, has beams which support the structure, and the wooden floor has been newly sanded and sealed. The new extension is now complete, below left. The wood has been freshly oiled and will soon blend in with the original structure.
(Michael Brandt)

73

7
grander restorations

Houses are built to live in and not to look on.

Of Building, FRANCIS BACON

For sheer one-upmanship the place to own is a manor house, and preferably one with a carved chimney-piece in the living-room and fine oak panelling with part of it shot-shattered where, during the Civil War, a Royalist was fired at while he was escaping. The episode, inscribed on the wall, bears witness to the fact. Elizabethan manor houses are full of history. Originally ornate village dwellings with elaborate timber-framed gables, they were where the rich and noble lord and his family held court over their tenants.

The manor houses, scattered through almost every county in England, make a collective group of noteworthy design in architecture. Says Sydney Jones in English Village Homes: "To them was applied the best work of the village craftsmen . . . these country houses present all the changes of style that came to domestic building over a long passage of years. By wall surfaces and roofs, gables, pediments and cornices, entrance doorways and porches, windows, chimneys, and other external particulars, they set forth the manifold ways in which every kind of building material was used towards making homes pleasant for living."

Even with their additions and alterations, therefore, (conversion being not only a twentieth-century prerogative) they still retain much of their original charm and character.

Campton Manor in Bedfordshire, from which the Royalist, Sir Charles Ventris, successfully made his getaway, was built in 1591 and is characteristically timber-framed with multi-gabled elevations. In the eighteenth century considerable extension and modification work was carried out to the rear of the house. The original staircase was replaced and the back rebuilt in brick to a classical Georgian design, including a semi-circular bay extension.

The domestic quarters were probably added after 1900, and much of the charm of the house derives from the diversity of architectural design between the individual rooms. A particular feature is the rood-screen which, in church architecture, is a screen which separates the nave from the choir. The date of the screen is believed to be c. 1600, and at some time it was incorporated into the main entrance hall. A minstrels' gallery, barrel-vaulted ceiling, open stone Tudor-arch fireplace, brick and tiled gazebo (a pretty little garden house) all contribute to the great charm of the manor.

Daintrey House in Sussex is an Elizabethan house with some late Stuart additions inside, and a Georgian façade. Its claim to fame is its description in the Sussex Archaeological Collections as "a sixteenth-century, timber-framed house Georgianised in the early eighteenth century". There is a magnificent Italian, plaster-carved ceiling in the drawing-room, and a fine Carolean staircase, presumably added about 1660–1668. The Tudor Room, in the Elizabethan portion of the house, is a stylish bedroom with fully panelled walls, leaded lights in the windows and a "duck's nest" grate in Sussex marble. Outside, the old bakehouse is used as a store.

Andrew Henderson describes the communal bakehouse with enormous oven that the lord of the manor provided for his tenants in his book, The Family House in England: "All tenants were required to use it, and a special licence was required to build any other oven. The baker rented it. His procedure was to fill it with faggots of wood which he then rekindled. The clay-lined interior retained sufficient heat for the rotational baking which followed the raking out of the embers. Flat oatmeal cakes could be baked on the hearthstone at home."

John Butterfield and Peter Gilbert, who run a country property restoration company, Butterfield Gilbert Country Properties Ltd., specialise in bringing old manor houses back to life. The Manor House in Toot Baldon near Oxford, once ecclesiastical and later belonging to The Queen's College, Oxford, is a splendid example of early Jacobean stone architecture, and an effective restoration job, in keeping with the original structure, has been carried out on it. When the manor was bought it was in a bad state of repair and a Victorian extension on the west side deprived most of the rooms of adequate light.

Records indicate that the Manor House was constructed in the middle of the sixteenth century from Cotswold stone brought down from quarries in and around Shipston-on-Stour. There were later additions in the seventeenth and eighteenth centuries, and in the Victorian era, when the fine westerly façade was defaced with a large brick extension, it must have been at the expense of several stone mullioned windows and an attractive central-gabled window.

The restoration was planned to redeem this original attractive face of the house and, from close examination of the old rough timbers and remnants of buried windows, the present façade looks much as it did in Jacobean times. The magnificent clusters of mellowed brick chimneys remain intact and all modern amenities, such as bathrooms, central heating and improved circulation, have been achieved, with the addition of only one small, new window.

The study is almost unchanged and retains the carved oak panelling which was installed in the seventeenth century by a Dr. Bacon, together with a unique stone font, in which over 150 children from adjoining villages were baptised.

The sensitive restoration was aimed at exposing all the original fireplaces, and re-introducing light to all rooms. The bumpy ceilings, sloping floors and the general flavour of a simple manor house have all been retained.

Small, cramped staircases were taken out, and the re-positioned stairway now provides easy access to the first and second floors, where all the vestiges of cramped attic rooms have been removed.

Downstairs there is now a hall with cloakroom, study, sitting-room, dining-room, kitchen with utility area, and a large walk-in larder. On the floors above are six bedrooms including master bedroom and guest suite and three bathrooms. The re-positioned front door incorporates a stone doorway brought down from a demolished house in Rutland.

Weekend retreats are not only a twentieth-century amenity. Asgill House in Richmond, Surrey was designed in the early 1760s by Sir Robert Taylor for the summer residence of Sir Charles Asgill, a merchant banker who had been Lord Mayor of London in 1757.

Situated by the River Thames on the site of the old Richmond Palace, it is a fine example of Georgian Palladian architecture. (Inigo Jones first introduced the work of Italian architect Andrea Palladio, 1508–80, into England in the early seventeenth century, and it did not become dominant until a century later.)

Described by various historians as "a little masterpiece of eighteenth-century architecture", and "remarkable for its chaste and simple elegance", the villa, once called Richmond Place, had a chequered history at the hands of various people who took on its conversion, and in the 1840s its size was approximately doubled.

The distinctive sloping roofs at the side of the house were raised to house servants, the basement being unusable because of flooding outside and in, and altogether the place had been thoroughly Victorianised.

By the time an American writer, Fred Hauptfuhrer, came to take it over in the late 1960s, Asgill House was a place of gaping floors, caving roofs, smashed interiors and the usual dank and dirt of a neglected, vandal-desecrated property. It has been restored to its former glory by Mr. Hauptfuhrer and his architect Donald Insall FRIBA, with the help of grants from the Historic Buildings Council and the Historic Buildings Board of the Greater London Council.

The downswept side roofs have been put back, their true pattern discovered by the plan shown on an engraving in the Ashmolean Museum, Oxford, and the beauty of the interior restored. Principal features are the two octagonal and oval rooms and the spiral staircase which comes up under one of the sloping side roofs. These oval rooms have cabinets and drawers built actually into the curves, so they are egg-shaped too!

One of the many problems of the whole carefully thought-out restoration which took two years, was that all the amenities had been concentrated in the Victorian additions which had been disposed of. There was no kitchen, bathroom or storage space, but now, with architectural ingenuity, one of the ground-floor reception rooms is a kitchen, and three bathrooms have been fitted in, one from a small anteroom leading into the master bedroom. Above all, the place is once more a family home, a house to be lived in.

The Dower House in Old Windsor, Berkshire, was built in Strawberry Hill Gothic, a strange assortment of styles, so called after Horace Walpole's Gothic decoration of Strawberry Hill, his house at Twickenham, Middlesex. The original Gothic architecture in the Middle Ages was full of heavy ornamentation, rich curves and arches, usually seen in ecclesiastical buildings.

This church-like decoration popped up again during the eighteenth and early nineteenth century. "A fashion for novels with a mediaeval setting produced a spontaneous effect upon architecture . . . house builders vied with each other in recreating 'Gothic' features of all descriptions," is how Hugh Braun effectively describes the whole scene in his book, Old English Houses.

A. L. Osborne goes a step further in English Domestic Architecture when he says: "Gothic was the chosen style and revivalism was born; a *soignée* melancholy was in the air, seen to be expressed by the Gothic poets and sham Gothic ruins".

111
The Dower House, with its typical pointed curve windows and iron glazing bars in fanciful patterns, certainly has the true Gothic flavour. It is pretty authentic, too, as, according to Mr. Osborne: "Aristocratic seats were enlarged and rebuilt in the Castle style, notably in Windsor *c.* 1826".

The place was used as a fodder store during the war and was partly restored in 1946 with bits and pieces from other houses, by Sir George Bellew KCB, then Garter King of Arms.

Timothy Tufnell, who restored it from a shell, has given it the full treatment. The entrance hall with its deep curving arch (the walls were down to the rough brick), has been replastered and painted pale orange and white. An original tiny half-curved window on the landing has been replaced by a full width and length one to give light on the stairway. The living-room has a central marble fireplace with deep pointed Gothic archways on either side which give a beautiful through room leading on to the garden.

XXIV
page 90
There is a double bathroom, divided only by natural wood louvre doors. The fittings, baths and basins, are plain white, in dramatic contrast to the rich art-nouveau style wallpaper in bright reds and blues, brown and black. A pretty guest-room has its own bathroom papered in a floral design to match the fabric used for curtains and divan covers.

As with many houses of that date, it faced north. Timothy Tufnell re-orientated the house, introducing a vine-shaded terrace on the south front, bounded by Gothic wrought-iron railings. This leads on to a paved formal garden and ornamental canal with ballet fountains and water lilies. Hidden in a miniature walled garden is the heated swimming pool with nearby Gothic-style changing-rooms.

112
"The property is a masterpiece of cottage architecture, scheduled as a building of local interest," is how Tayling's Holiday Cottages' catalogue describes a Gothic-style shooting lodge at Crieff in Scotland, one of a wide selection of traditional and unusual properties to rent for holiday periods in Britain. This particular holidaymaker's dream was built about 1810 in the rugged setting of moor, waterfall and hill, with fishing (boat provided) in a small trout loch nearby. It has been converted to luxury standards,

103 (right)
Campton Manor in Bedfordshire is an Elizabethan manor house with, far right, a characteristically timber-framed exterior with multi-gabled elevations. In the eighteenth century considerable work was carried out to the rear of the house, right, including the addition of a semi-circular bay.

104 (below right)
Daintrey House in Petworth, Sussex is a sixteenth-century, timber-framed house which was added to and modified in the eighteenth century. The picture of the rear of the house shows the original Elizabethan portion on the left, together with the Georgian façade.

and has night storage heaters, telephone and television. What more could you want for secluded vacation recreation?

The Logs in Hampstead, North London looks, from the outside, like four separate houses. "First there is the Victorian Church portion on the left, then the Norman Provincial followed by the French Château tower portion and finally Misbegotten Palladian," wrote architect C. Bernard Brown in his book, The Conversion of Old Buildings Into New Houses.

"That the architect was able to sort out this welter of styles into six houses reflects considerable credit on him. The Victorian habit of building well helped to give substantial party walls and, in replanning, living-rooms were kept away from the bedrooms of adjoining units. Externally very little was done, which was wise, as the property will remain as a unique example of the grand middle-class house of 1867."

Existing materials were used wherever possible. Three fireplaces were formed with slate from the larder shelves and balusters for staircases formed with twisted burglar bars from the windows. The existing doors were re-used wherever possible and some radiators were tested and found serviceable.

As it was such a strongly built house, breeze blocks were used for new partitions, which made planning more flexible on the upper floors, as they did not have to be supported by the ground-floor partitions.

105, 106
Restoration of The Manor House in Toot Baldon near
Oxford was planned to bring back to life the original face of
this sixteenth-century house. The building now looks very
much as it did in Jacobean times, and the new stonework
round the middle section, above, will soon weather into a
similar colour to the old stonework.

107, 108, 109
*Asgill House in Richmond, Surrey, built on the site of the
old Richmond Palace, is a fine example of Georgian
Palladian architecture. Designed in the early 1760s it had a
chequered history at the hands of many people who took on
its conversion, and in the 1840s its size was almost doubled.
By the time it was taken over for restoration in the late 1960s
it had gaping floors, caving roofs and smashed interiors, below.
Its true shape was discovered on a plan in the Ashmolean
Museum in Oxford, right, and this plan was followed
to restore the house to the place it is today, below right.
(Greater London Council)*

Elevation and Plan of the PRINCIPAL STORY of the Villa
Built for the late Sir Charles Asgill Bart at Richmond

110
*Strawberry Hill Gothic, a strange assortment of styles, is
so called after Horace Walpole's Gothic decoration of
Strawberry Hill, his house at Twickenham, Middlesex,
built in the eighteenth century. The above is from a drawing
by William Maplow.
(Victoria and Albert Museum)*

111 (below)
The Dower House in Old Windsor, Berkshire, is a splendid
example of Strawberry Hill Gothic, with its curved,
ecclesiastical-style windows and ornamental glazing bars,
and deep curving arch over the front entrance. The small,
turreted tower on the right is an imitation of the original
Strawberry Hill residence.

112 (above)
"A masterpiece of cottage architecture", is how Tayling's Holiday Cottages' catalogue describes this Gothic-style shooting lodge in Crieff, Scotland. Built about 1810 in a setting of moors, waterfalls and hills, with a nearby trout loch, it has been converted into a luxury holiday home.
(Alex C. Cowper)

113, 114 (right)
The Logs in Hampstead, London, which looks from the outside like four separate houses, above right, is described by architect, C. Bernard Brown, as having a Victorian church portion on the left, followed by the Norman Provincial, French Château and finally Misbegotten Palladian. In its conversion to six attractive dwellings the exterior has not been changed and existing materials have been used wherever possible. The lofty apartment, below right, has a large, open-plan room with the kitchen off to the left, and sleeping quarters in the gallery above.
(Millar and Harris)

8
work buildings with a future

A forted residence 'gainst the tooth of time
And razure of oblivion.

Measure for Measure, WILLIAM SHAKESPEARE

115 It is not only old barns that have a fascination for restorers. Fortress and tower, coach house and chapel, all have their appeal for conversion to residential use.

On Alderney in the Channel Islands, Fort Corblets is one of the oldest and finest fortresses on the island. Built of granite, it has been skilfully enlarged and converted to provide gracious living. This includes an observation room with magnificent picture windows over the rocky coastline, a Moroccan garden-room with ornamental pool and fountain, a bistro room for parties, a wine store and a 90 feet (27·4 metres) long greenhouse.

Equally interesting is another kind of fortress which has been cleverly converted into a seaside retreat. Architect Ronald Ward, designer of one of London's newer landmarks, the 35-storey Millbank Tower, spends his weekends in a rather different kind of tower – a Martello Tower.

116 This is on West Parade, Hythe in Kent, a sturdy circular building like the base of a lighthouse, standing at the edge of the sea, on which a passerby was heard to comment: "Fancy anyone being daft enough to *build* a house like that!"

These towers go back over a century and a half and originated in Corsica. They were built in Britain to ward off seaborne attacks at the time of Napoleon and are now essentially a feature of the South East. Of the original 74 in Kent and Sussex and 29 in Essex and Suffolk, only 28 and 18 respectively remain, plus a few in the Orkneys and Eire. Those on the South Coast were numbered 1 to 74, while those on the East Coast were lettered.

The round towers, originally costing from around £2,000 to £3,000 each to build, had no utility services laid on, and the interiors were gloomy and unwholesome. To seaward they present an unbroken expanse of brickwork finished with stucco, while at the rear is an entrance reached by a ladder, plus two small windows on the landward side.

The towers are, in fact, slightly elliptical. The external walls at beach level (and they go down deeper than that) are 13 feet 6 inches (4·1 metres)

thick, reducing to 9 feet (2·7 metres) at the top on the seaward side and 5 feet (1·5 metres) at the rear. The parapet is about 34 feet (10·4 metres) above the lower floor level, while the average width of the tower is just over 40 feet (12·2 metres) around. Sometimes they were surrounded by a moat which was crossed by a drawbridge.

On the roof of the Wards' tower was a 24-pounder cannon bearing the initials of George III, dated 1824. It now sits like a watchdog in the forecourt on the second carriage provided. These cannon were supported on a brick column 5 feet (1·5 metres) in diameter, running from the base, which also supported all the floors and joists radiating from it.

There are over three quarters of a million bricks to a tower, sufficient to build 70 good-sized houses. The bricks are set in lime, ash and hot tallow, and to remove any portion of the building needs drills. It took two men three weeks with a compressor and two drill guns to make a wardrobe!

The Wards' Martello was sold by the War Department in 1906 to a private family, when the Hythe sea-wall was erected. It changed hands again in 1928 when it was converted into three apartments, and was sold again in 1937 and requisitioned during the last war as an observation post for the guns firing on Calais.

Mrs. Ward bought it in 1960, the year after her husband was commissioned to design the new Dungeness Lighthouse (the first lighthouse to be built in Britain for 53 years), which can be seen from the sitting-room window.

The lower ground floor at moat level, is a self-contained housekeeper's apartment of living-room and two bedrooms. The middle floor has the entrance hall, dining-room and kitchen, plus the guest suite, the bathroom of which was carved out of the thickness of the wall.

The upper floor consists of the sitting-room and the Wards' bedroom suite. The feature of this section is the large sitting-room: it is like being on the bridge of a ship, for it overlooks the English Channel on two sides. The bedroom overlooks a pretty rockery garden at the rear, and on the roof is an air-conditioned sun-room leading on to a tiled patio.

The kitchen created one of the major headaches, because there is no upright wall and the floor and ceiling are out of parallel. A grid was used based on a 12¾ inch (32·4 cm) module to enable the pieces of domestic equipment to be planned into its irregular perimeter. Now the kitchen houses a waste disposal unit, grill and oven, refrigerator, deep freeze, in fact, every labour-saving device you can think of – even the refuse bin opens by remote control!

In the 1920s water towers were built to service isolated housing estates, and one that became obsolete in Sussex in the 1950s when main water services were brought in, was converted by an artist for living and working in. On the outside it remained the same, tall and imposing, 60 feet (18·3 metres) high, but inside it became a fascinating home and studio.

The foreman who superintended the building of the tower claimed that there were 2,300 nuts and bolts used in its construction, and he swears he had to go round tightening each one! A passageway at the bottom of the tower was transformed into a small sitting-room and the room leading off it which used to house the machinery to operate the tower became a studio. There is a minute "cupboard" of a kitchen, a dining alcove with white-washed brick walls, and upstairs there is a bedroom and bathroom.

A coach house and a bell tower – what a marvellous combination for conversion. Rosemary Borland had both in the grounds of her eighteenth-century house in Essex and both were on the point of falling in. The roof sagged, the bell tower had a precarious lean to it and, at the back, whole panels of walling had cracked and settled at a variety of angles.

The coach house had nine rooms above the stables (two loose boxes and two stalls) where the gardeners and the stable boys lived, as well as the groom and coachman. Some leather boots were found in the woodshed, which were once worn by the pony pulling the lawn-mower to prevent hoof-marks on the turf!

The stabling has been left exactly as it was, with the coach space for garaging, and living accommodation, one large sitting-room, kitchen, bedroom with bathroom, guest room with shower and lavatory, all restricted to the first floor.

As much as possible of the original material was salvaged and used again in the restoration, such as iron hinges and latches for doors, bricks from derelict cowsheds (which had fallen down a long time ago) for walls, and old tiles from the roof. Trees which had to be chopped down to make way for new wiring were sawn into floor boards.

The existing circular and oval windows on the front were ripped out and remade. At the back, new window openings were formed to coincide with those at the front. The rather odd brickwork led the owner to believe there had been round or oval-shaped windows there in the first place.

The whole place has been ingeniously restored. The bell rings again on the tower, and the clock winding mechanism comes up from the stable through the first-floor living-room. The chains and weights have been enclosed in a glass box.

The whole operation was master-minded by Rosemary Borland with the aid of architect John Amor and builder S. A. Mills. Mrs. Borland did all the interior design, and the step-by-step photographs which tell the story so effectively were taken by her son-in-law, Stephen Moreton-Prichard.

Another fascinating building – a tower with a coach house attached – is Tower House in London's Park Village West. Designed by John Nash (1752–1835) who, as architect to George IV, built Buckingham Palace, it has been described as a small, classical villa with an octagonal tower and broad-eaved roof, and the most entertaining and charming in the village.

The first tenant was Dr. James Johnson, physician to the Duke of Clarence; more recently it was lived in by Woodrow Wyatt, writer and former British Member of Parliament. Mr. Wyatt commissioned architect John Burkett of Scarlett Burkett Associates to join up the coach house to the main house to give extra accommodation.

The house itself, although it looks big from the outside, has a lot of wasted space – landings and a "dancing" staircase take up a great deal of room. Below street level (at garden level at the back) is a large kitchen, bathroom, separate lavatory, wine cellar and good-sized dining-room with French windows leading on to the terrace. The tower room below street level was converted into a tiny office. From this floor the staircase leads up to a wide landing/hall, large drawing-room with balcony leading down to the terrace and study (also large and leading on to the balcony) and the octagonal hall in the tower at street level, with front door to the street. The staircase continues up to the next wide landing and one large bedroom, with dressing-room, bathroom and lavatory. The small octagonal room over the

122

123

124

125

126

87

front hall is really too small for anything in the way of a good-sized bedroom although it could be used for the occasional overnight guest. A tiny winding staircase leads up to the top tower room under the sloping ceiling.

Converting the coach house and joining it on to the main house provided the extra rooms that were needed. The front part of the coach house was left at its original level, but an open gallery was added, with stairs up, for storage space.

At the back, part of the floor was lowered to allow for two downstairs rooms and to give enough height for a second floor, with good wardrobe space on the landing, a kitchen and a living-room. There is a bathroom at ground level, just inside from the door to the garage, and one of the two main rooms at ground level is used as a bedroom, the other as an office. The passageway joining the conversion to the old house has two stairways, one down to the back door and kitchen, the other a few wooden steps up to the study, through a "secret" door which is part of the bookshelves on the study side. By the side of the bookcases in the passageway a door leads to a large "party" room – also newly added – lead-
127 ing on to the terrace by the side of the study.

128 New homes for the horses was the aim of Robert Barlow, when he was planning to convert the coach house and stables of De Vere Mews in London's Royal Borough of Kensington.

About 100 years ago, the land for the mews was bought by a family called Daw, who built the mews as coach houses on the ground floor, stables on the first and grooms' living quarters on the second. The coming of the motor-car naturally meant the coach houses were turned into garages but because one of the family was particularly attached to horses, the stables on the first floor were retained.
129, 130 Now that De Vere Mews and the adjacent Canning Place Mews are being integrated by the Barlow Cannon Estates into one complex, the horses of the Civil Service Riding Club (tenants for over 14 years) are to be rehoused at basement level. "A much better idea," claim the residents, who have been kept awake at night by the horses turning over!

Pym Gate House was originally a coaching inn on Pym's Way in Cheshire about 300 years ago. The word "gate" had an earlier meaning of "way", with Pym being, incidentally, an anti-Royalist statesman in Charles I's time.

The house had been altered and added to over the years, and the oldest part of the building was so full of dry rot that Ashley Larmuth and his wife who brought the place back to life had,

reluctantly, to have this part demolished. That left them with a Victorianised bay-windowed front (the windows were falling away from the brick, leaving a 6-inch, 15·2 cm, gap), and a back with a small, round, tower-style wing.

The verandah, which had been added at the back, had broken glass, rotten frames and, as it was of very little use since that side of the property faced north and east, it was taken down. Its removal greatly accentuated the grace of the castellated tower.

"The house was in a pitiful state – condemned as unfit for human habitation," said the Larmuths. "It had water in the cellar 6 feet (1·8 metres) deep, there was dry rot round the front door, and a creeper had crept not only over the front, but right round the insides of the rooms. The walls were mouldy and the floors were wet with damp. It smelt horrible."

Yet these obstacles did not seem to deter them. Long battles with the gas company, problems over the central-heating installation, coping with a stream under the cellar, all these problems were overcome to produce a gracious elegant home, as you can see in the photographs taken by Mrs. Larmuth.

Another coach house and bell tower, the Coach House, Courtwick Park near Littlehampton in Sussex, was also in an extremely dilapidated condition before its conversion.

A small, late eighteenth, possibly early nineteenth century building, built in Strawberry Hill Gothic style, the knapped flint walls with exquisite "galleting" (a surface finish of small stones pressed into a mortar joint while it is still soft), it was believed to have been used as a coach house until the turn of the century. As it was gradually slipping into a state of decay – roof falling in, window mouldings crumbling, and the whole place overgrown with foliage – a full-scale rescue operation had to be carried out.

Only the original walls and parts of the roof were of any use in the restoration, and although a fine king post roof truss was retained, the remainder of the roof structure had to be

XXII, XXIII
Roma Jay's kitchen after conversion. The new split-level oven has been built into a recessed wall, top right, the larder has been knocked down and replaced by planned storage, and shelves to take cookery books have been built in. A new twin sink has been installed by the side of the cooker, below right, and shelving and storage cupboards have been fitted on the opposite wall. The vinyl blinds on the door and window match the wallcovering, and the tiles over the sink pick up perfectly the orange in the vinyl and paintwork.
(Jay Kitchen Consultants)

XXIV
The Dower House in Old Windsor, Berkshire, recently restored from a shell by Timothy Tufnell, has been given the full treatment. The double bathroom, divided by natural wood louvre doors, has been dramatically decorated in bright reds and blues, brown and black.
(Brian Morris)

replaced. The original quatrefoil windows (their shape like a four leaf clover, was actually a Gothic symbol for the cross and the four evengelists) were rebuilt. The problem was how to open these unusual styled windows. The solution was provided by inward opening casements set behind the stone dressings.

Another difficulty was the replacement of a stone band course at eaves level on the front of the house which had several sections missing, as well as being in an advanced state of decay.

"We had some of the similar dressings at the back removed, and re-used them on the front," explained Euan Crowther of the Building Design Department of King and Chasemore, who prepared detailed working drawings of the attractive conversion.

The original stable area was made into a large living-room, and the coach houses at each end were converted into a kitchen in the north wing, and an entrance hall, a study-bedroom and cloakroom in the south side. A spiral staircase goes up to two bedrooms and a bathroom. The idea of having a spiral was that it was essential to keep the stair-well opening in such a position that the first floor layout related to the existing window openings.

The clock below the bell tower had its face repainted and new hands fitted; the bell is also the original one, dating back to Battle of Trafalgar days, 1805. Alas, the mechanism is gone, so it is purely decorative.

115
Towers, too, have their appeal for conversion to residential use. This one is a wing of an old house in the Dordogne district of France and was probably once part of the buildings belonging to the nearby seventeenth-century château. (Trevor Kenyon)

116, 117
Architect Ronald Ward and his wife spend their weekends in
a converted Martello Tower in Hythe, Kent, complete with a
cannon in the forecourt bearing the initials of George III.
Before its conversion it was a forbidding-looking round tower,
a mini-fortress, built of three-quarters of a million bricks, to
ward off seaborne attacks at the time of Napoleon. Now the
tower has every amenity necessary to luxury living – there
is even an air-conditioned sun-room on the roof, leading to a
tiled patio, right, where Mr. Ward can look out to the
French coast.

118
The feature of the upper floor of the Martello Tower is the large sitting-room which is like being on the bridge of a ship, because it overlooks the English Channel on two sides. The study bay, cocktail bar and cupboards have been carved out of the walls which are about 9 feet thick.
(Jack C. Adams)

119

The back of the Coach House before its conversion with a sagging roof, whole panels of walling cracked and the bell tower leaning precariously. Left a little longer the whole structure might have fallen in.
(Stephen Moreton-Prichard)

120
*The front of the eighteenth-century Coach House before its
conversion showing the leaning bell tower.
(Stephen Moreton-Prichard)*

121 (above)
The interior of the Coach House was in just as bad a state as the outside. Wood was rotting and brickwork crumbling. (Stephen Moreton-Prichard)

122 (below)
The front of the Coach House after its conversion. The coach doors have been replaced but are still in keeping with the originals. The circular and oval windows were ripped out and remade, and the old tiles, carefully removed from the roof by the builders, were re-used. (Stephen Moreton-Prichard)

123, 124, 125
Detail of the Coach House, above left, shows the new round window at the rear. The rather odd brickwork – the first of its kind the bricklayers had ever tackled – led the owner to believe there had been round or oval-shaped windows there in the first place. The door to the woodshed, above, comes from a local inn which was being demolished and the licence of the publican, Cornelius Aylward remains, rescued by the owner of the Coach House, Rosemary Borland. The whole place has been ingeniously restored. The bell rings again on the tower and the clock winding mechanism, which comes up from the stable through the first-floor living-room, left, is enclosed in a glass cage.
(Stephen Moreton-Prichard)

126, 127 (right)
One of London's most fascinating buildings is Tower House in Park Village West, above right. Designed by John Nash, architect to George IV, the coach house was recently joined on to the main house to provide the extra accommodation needed. A glassed-in gallery, below right, which joins the coach house to Tower House, also serves as a party room.
(Gordon McLeish)

128, 129, 130

Plans have recently been made for the conversion of De Vere Mews in London's Royal Borough of Kensington to provide new homes for the horses of the Civil Service Riding Club. The original coach houses, now garages, below, are on street level, the stables are on the first floor – there is hay for the horses' feed at the end of the mews – and the grooms' living quarters are on the second floor. The proposed conversion includes the integrating of De Vere Mews, above right, with adjacent Canning Place Mews, below right. The original balconies of De Vere Mews are being retained, together with all the best architectural features of the mews. The horses' stables are being rebuilt in the basement, below right, and on the left of the picture the backs of the residences fronting on De Vere Mews are where the original coach houses and stables used to be. In the far background is a three-storey Georgian town house and office block, and in the foreground is a wide ramp leading to an underground car park with space for 108 cars.

(Sydney Newbery)

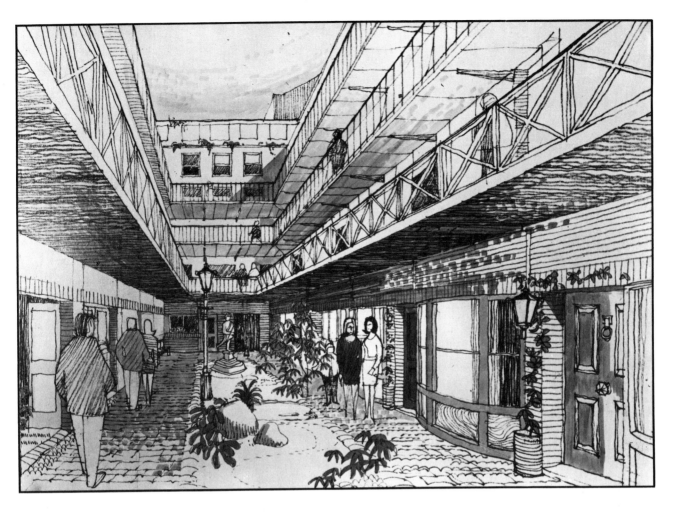

101

131, 132
Pym Gate House, originally a coaching inn in Cheshire before conversion, above. On the left is the 300-year-old part, next to it is the section added about 100 years later and on the right the largest part, including the front door, was added a further century after. The Victorian bay windows were built on to the front but not keyed in, so they fell away in time, leaving a 6-inch gap. At the back of the house, below, was a small, round, tower-style wing and a dilapidated verandah. (Ashley Larmuth)

133, 134

The removal of the verandah at the rear of the house, left, revealed the grace of the castellated tower, and new windows were fitted to be in keeping with the style of the front ones. Long, narrow windows each side of the French doors were replaced with those with similar glazing bars and the top, curved, sash window was replaced in its original style. The creeper was cut away from the front of the house, below, to expose the elegant façade, with gently curving windows taking the place of the ground-floor bays. The oldest part of the building had, regrettably, to be demolished, as it did not survive the conversion. There is a new doorway, new top and side windows, and the garden of nettles, brambles, old bicycles, bedsteads and rubbish has been cleared to reveal the beauty of the giant fir tree.
(Ashley Larmuth)

135 (above)
A full-scale rescue operation had to be carried out on The
Coach House near Littlehampton in Sussex. Built in
Strawberry Hill Gothic style in the late eighteenth century,
it had more recently been neglected – the roof was falling in,
window mouldings crumbling and the place was overgrown.
(Euan Crowther)

136 (below)
Only the original walls and part of the roof were of any use
in the restoration. The original quatrefoil windows were
completely rebuilt and the coach houses at each end were
converted into a kitchen in the north wing and an entrance
hall, a study-bedroom and cloakroom in the south side.
(Ron Oulds)

137
It was essential to have a spiral staircase to keep the stair-well
opening in such a position that the first-floor layout related to
the existing window openings.
(Ron Oulds)

9
and still more besides...

There was no leaf upon the forest bare,
No flower upon the ground,
And little motion in the air
Except the mill-wheel's sound.

Charles the First, PERCY BYSSHE SHELLEY

Whether the mill-wheel is still there or not, and whether the mill is in Périgord or Somerset, the attraction of living in a converted watermill seems to have particular appeal.

I have always felt that the place to go for watermills in abundance is Portugal. There are over 25,000 in different parts of the country. The vast number is explained by the fact that until recently each peasant ground his own corn. Nowadays Portuguese watermills are mostly used for irrigation, but what splendid opportunities there must be for domestic conversion!

Back in Britain, I found the Your Cottage in the Country people carrying out what they claimed to be "the most difficult, yet challenging and exciting conversion we have so far undertaken". They were referring to Low Mill in Grassington, Wharfedale, Yorkshire, which was an old flour mill in the National Park.

The building looked pretty dilapidated when I first saw it, but work was underway to convert it into a four-storey house of character and distinction. Because of the slope down to the water, the two lower floors on the side facing the river are below ground level, whereas the third and fourth floors are above ground level all round. This makes it very convenient for access to the building, because two floors are above and two below the main entrance.

The first floor contains a study and a library. On the second floor is the nursery/playroom with its own separate entrance for the children, a long gallery giving access to a balcony which overlooks the river, and a storage room. The third floor provides the major living area and the main entrance to the house. There is also a hall and cloakroom, living and dining areas which have special lighting arrangements for displaying china, and a kitchen with laundry-room.

The fourth floor is the dormitory one with the master bedroom suite which leads to a dressing-room complete with mirrors and wardrobe space and its own green bathroom. The inner corridor entered from a door on the landing is particularly interesting with a barrel-vaulted ceiling. It also serves to isolate the suite from the rest of the family. Two single bedrooms, one double bedroom and a blue bathroom complete the area.

Another mill, which was still in use as a flour mill until about two years ago, although, of course, electric power was used in recent years, is Littlebourne Water Mill in Canterbury. Listed as being of special architectural interest, an account of a mill on the same site is mentioned in the Domesday Book, 1086. However, the present building was originally constructed in the eighteenth century.

It has been completely renovated, skilfully preserving all the important and interesting features, at the same time creating a spacious modern home of exceptional character. The structure has been virtually rebuilt with many new or strengthened main timbers, entirely new external weatherboarding, new roof timbers and tiling. Internally, the walls were lined with non-combustible insulating material, and the floors were re-surfaced. The original waterwheel was repaired and the wheelhouse rebuilt.

Bleadney Mill in North Somerset, one of the oldest water-powered mills (the site is in the Domesday records too) had been abandoned for 25 years when Leonard Taylor and his wife bought it. It was full of farm equipment and chickens, and the wheel had not ground corn for many years.

XXV (top right)
The passion for doing up country property can be indulged in to complete satisfaction in the Dordogne district of France. (European Property Services)

XXVI (below right)
John and Elizabeth Belsey live in this attractive, early nineteenth-century, converted farmhouse overlooking three acres of meadow in Siorac de Ribérac in the Dordogne. (Burton and Evans)

138

139

The main structure of the roof was sound, but it had to be stripped to renew battens and tiles before the original tiles were replaced. On an inside wall was a blocked-in window arch immediately above the granary door. An enterprising miller at one time must have built up the land at the right hand end of the building to the level of the rising road, so that grain could be delivered direct into the first floor without all the bother of hoisting through the opening.

The window was opened up again after excavating the earth around it. The huge, open spaces of the two warehouses were divided into rooms, with the partitions fitting neatly with the existing beams.

After the living quarters were organised – hall, dining and living-rooms, cloakroom and kitchen on the ground floor, three bedrooms, bathroom, workroom and "hobby" room on the first floor – Leonard Taylor, who has his own engineering works, determined to get the mill wheels going again, this time to produce electricity. The original waterwheel had collapsed through rust and was bogged down by weeds. The iron rims and axle shaft were in good condition and, with new steel buckets and oak spokes, the wheel was ready for use again.

Inside the mill, cast-iron gears with apple-wood teeth were mounted on a heavy vertical shaft, once part of a ship's mast. As the overshot water-wheel gathered the water of the old mill stream, the power turned the huge dovetailing gears to drive the cumbersome millstones on the floor above. Enough revs per minute are produced by the great wheel churning the water to generate all the electricity needed for light and heating.

Bassingbourn Mill in Hertfordshire, the main part of which was built in 1800, has been skilfully converted. The mill was made into the main residence with five bedrooms, two bathrooms and four reception rooms. The two adjacent rolling mills were converted into two self-contained apartments, the granary provided a magnificent studio/gallery 75 feet (22·9 metres) long, with garaging for six cars at ground floor level and the stables have become a cottage.

The mill-wheel and stream are illuminated by 10 external lights, making it a magnificent sight at night.

A property I would have loved to have had a go at converting, was an old dilapidated sawmill I saw in Kerry, Montgomeryshire. The estate agent's particulars described it as a stone and slated building of character, and I had to agree. The setting was quiet and rural, with only the faint babbling of the water in the nearby brook. I just hope that whoever bought it (there was outline planning consent for conversion to a dwelling) didn't knock it down.

144

Now that farmers don't need so many oasts, the distinctive buildings are being converted to live in. In Kent, the Weald of Kent Preservation Society are very particular about what you do with your oast. They want to maintain the original character by painting the cowl white and the kiln roof-line uninterrupted by windows.

145

Built around 1850, Four Kiln Oast, now called The Roundels, is a classic example of many Kentish round oasts set in the heart of the Weald. It was a working oast until it was converted and, unlike so many, escaped the period of deterioration which makes modernisation so difficult.

146

Mrs. Diana De Morgan created a spacious and comfortable home from the barn of the oast, (then 81 feet, 24·7 metres, long), plus the three roundels and a square kiln, all giving a tremendous amount of space. It was decided to demolish part of the original barn area and build a new end wall and chimney with a large open fireplace of old brick. The demolition also made it necessary to construct a new roof, using the original tiles and, to balance this, one roundel was shortened. This left a large 51 feet by 30 feet (15·5 metres by 9·1 metres) sitting-room, and facilities for a kitchen, dining-room and another sitting-room in the remaining roundels, plus space for a cloakroom. The dining-room has a ceiling 15 feet (4·6 metres) high, specially kept when the oast was partly demolished.

Upstairs there are two round bedrooms and a guest bathroom. The main suite consists of a very large bedroom on two levels with adjoining bathroom and dressing-room. The charm of this house is the entrance opening straight into the living-room with its Danish pine floor, unique spiral staircase and circular landing. The garden is about half an acre and the more modern oast has been made into a large garage and workshop.

The present owners, Mr. and Mrs. Paul Knill Jones, are still adding their own finishing touches to what must be one of the most delightful and well designed oast conversions in Kent.

A slaughterhouse for a home? Why not? Saltings in Egloshayle, Wadebridge, Cornwall was built as a farm slaughterhouse about 100 years ago immediately adjacent to a cemetery, and during recent years it fell into disrepair and became semi-derelict, finally being used as a grain store.

Arthur Dongray, a talented local artist, and his wife Barbara, an accomplished worker in fabric collage, were perceptive enough to see the possibilities of the site, and the suitability of the building for conversion to a home and studio.

The stone shell was carefully gutted, and the front walls and various roofs removed; conversion works were then contained within the three remaining walls. All the old stone was re-used and the reformed roofs covered with the old slates. Living accommodation is concentrated on the ground floor, and a studio has been formed within the roof space with an open gallery over the dining area. The clever conversion was designed by Roy W. Sale ARIBA.

The studio-cottage is called Saltings because it overlooks to the south a pleasant green valley known locally as the Saltings, through which the Camel river flows on its way to Padstow and the sea. A floor-length window gives the sitting-room the full benefit of this outlook. There are no windows on the north side, because the view would be an extension of the churchyard. Clerestory windows, which are windows placed near the top of a wall above an adjacent roof, were fitted to give the studio the necessary north light.

The centre of the house and the stairs are effectively lit by a large, domed, double-skinned, Perspex roof light set high above the dining recess, where it also pleasantly emphasises the texture of an area of unrendered stonework in the back wall. All the ground belonging to the Dongrays is in the sunny front, and a sliding aluminium door leads out on to a patio which is sheltered by walls on three sides.

The cost of conversion was kept within an initial budget figure and, although local craftsmen did the bulk of the work to the architect's supervision, the Dongrays carried out their own interior decoration, including treating with seal all the pine used for structural beams, ceilings and kitchen service divider. Instead of plaster, walls were finished with a sponged cement render – a one-coat treatment for economy which gives a very pleasant texture.

A Methodist Chapel converted to a small house is another adventurous conversion that was taken on by the Your Cottage in the Country people. Now called Whistling Green at Crayke, near Easingwold, York, they bought the chapel complete with curved and pointed ecclesiastical glass windows, bell tower and pews. Alas, all these church-style appendages had to go to make the conversion a viable proposition.

Modern windows were fitted into the front of the building, the bell tower was replaced by garage, sun deck and external staircase, and the pews were removed to give living space.

On the ground floor are the dining-hall, cloakroom, kitchen where the old vestry was, three bedrooms and a bathroom. On the first floor, approached by an open pine staircase, is the large sitting-room and another bedroom with bathroom attached. The location of the latter is in the north-east corner of the chapel at the pulpit end.

The original boarded ceiling and roof trusses were kept and varnished to give a lofty, arched effect to the sitting-room. The sun deck was built in such a way that a *belvedere* could be constructed on the low parapet wall. (*Belvedere* is Italian for beautiful view. In Italian Renaissance architecture it referred to the uppermost storey of a building which was open at several sides to allow for viewing the countryside, or to let in the cooling breeze.)

147

148

138
Moulin de Vesignol, built by a stream called Le Boulanger in Périgord, France, is an old mill house awaiting conversion. At the moment there are just two rooms and a kitchen with a fireplace and exposed beams. It has been suggested that the old millstone room should be the sitting-room, a nearby canal a swimming-pool and the old barn and oven-room should form the rest of the accommodation.

139 (above)
Low Mill in Grassington, Yorkshire, once a flour mill in the
National Park, was in a bad state of disrepair before its
conversion to a four-storey house.
(John Gresswell)

140 (right)
Up until two years ago Littlebourne Water Mill in
Canterbury was still in use as a flour mill. A mill on the
same site as this one is mentioned in the Domesday Book but
the present building was constructed in the eighteenth century.
It has been completely renovated but all the important and
interesting features have been preserved, including the original
waterwheel and the wheelhouse.
(Ben May)

141, 142
Bleadney Mill in North Somerset, one of the oldest water-powered mills in the country, above, had been abandoned for 25 years when it was bought for conversion. Today it is a three-bedroomed home, right, with its own electricity – generated by the old waterwheel brought back into use.

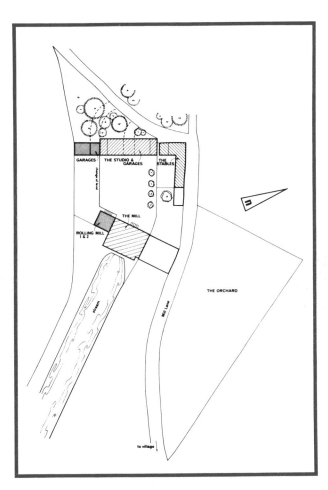

143 (left)
The plan shows how Bassingbourn Mill in Hertfordshire was converted. The mill was made into the main residence with five bedrooms, the two adjacent rolling mills were converted into two self-contained apartments, the granary provided space for a studio/gallery with garages at ground level and the stables have become a cottage.

144 (below)
I would have loved to have had a go at converting this old sawmill that I saw in Kerry, Montgomeryshire. It was a stone and slated building set in beautiful countryside – the only sound around was the babbling of a nearby brook.
(Trevor Kenyon)

113

145, 146
Four Kiln Oast, above, now called The Roundels, is a classic example of Kentish round oasts. Built about 1850, it was a working oast up until the time it was bought for conversion. Now The Roundels is a spacious home, below. The barn was used for the main body of the house, with other accommodation in the roundels, and the more modern square kiln became a large garage and workshop. Part of the original barn area was demolished during the conversion which made it necessary to construct a new roof, using the original tiles, and, to balance this, one of the roundels was shortened.
(Paul Knill Jones)

147, 148
Saltings in Cornwall was originally built as a farm slaughterhouse about 100 years ago, next to a cemetery. During recent years it became semi-derelict until it was taken over and converted into a studio-cottage. The rear backs on to the cemetery, above, while the front looks over a valley called the Saltings, below. The floor-length window gives the sitting-room the full benefit of this view. The exterior of the house combines stone, slate and treated boarding, all an effective foil to the unusual shaped windows.

149, 150 (left)
Another adventurous conversion taken on by Your Cottage in the Country Ltd. was a Methodist Chapel. Now called Whistling Green at Crayke near Easingwold, York, the chapel was bought complete with curved and pointed ecclesiastical glass windows, bell tower and pews, inset.

151,152
Most of the church-style appendages had to go during the conversion. Modern windows were fitted into the front of the building, above, and the bell tower was replaced by a sun deck over a garage, below. The sun deck was built in such a way that a belvedere (Italian for a beautiful view) could be constructed on the low parapet wall.

10
cottages international

*Better the shabby building which is also part of the landscape
than the brash modern construction which seems to shriek:
"Notice me, I am new".*

Do You Care About Historic Buildings? COUNTESS OF DARTMOUTH

Cottages and conversions are international, a revolt against the concrete jungles that seem to spring up almost overnight. Gradually, however, concerted efforts are being made to build new houses in traditional, graceful style, as well as to bring new life to old cottages.

The Countess of Dartmouth's introduction to the book Do You Care About Historic Buildings? about the conservation and restoration of houses, cottages, grander buildings and the like in London and its environs, is just as appropriate to buildings all over the world. She says: "We live in an age clouded by violence, noise and ugliness; sporadic violence stabs at the fragile fabric of our civilisation; noise jars our ears and our senses; ugliness, sadly so often part of modern art, architecture and music, shocks rather than soothes, frightens rather than calms the soul.

"Assailed on all sides by these threats to any peace of mind, people cling more and more to the familiar and loved. Better the old teddy bear with the missing ear than the spiky new model of the space-ship. Better the shabby building which is also part of the landscape than the brash modern construction which seems to shriek: 'Notice me, I am new'."

The following illustrations of places old and new should speak for themselves.

153
New high buildings – apartment blocks and hotels – form a concrete jungle which is gradually encroaching on the green belt in Spain.
(Trevor Kenyon)

154 (above)
The old: an apartment block near Alicante in Spain awaits conversion or demolition.
(Trevor Kenyon)

155 (below)
The new: this apartment block by the sea at La Cala near Alicante in Spain is well landscaped with palm trees.
(Trevor Kenyon)

158 (below)
Casa Menette near Moraira in Spain is a contemporary style villa with a difference – it has an interior patio with pool. The main rooms are on the ground floor and on the first floor is the third bedroom and a bathroom. A large roof terrace completes the half circle.

159 (right)
The traditional Spanish style has been copied in the building of this village of 38 apartments at Cuarton near Algeciras. (Frederick Ayer)

156 (above)
This new but traditional style villa with terrace is situated at El Tosalet, Javea, Spain.
(Trevor Kenyon)

157 (below)
The plan of this new but traditional style villa at Finca Campello near Alicante in Spain shows how neatly everything dovetails on one floor – patio and terrace, lounge, dining-room off the kitchen, and two bedrooms, one with bathroom and the other with a shower room.

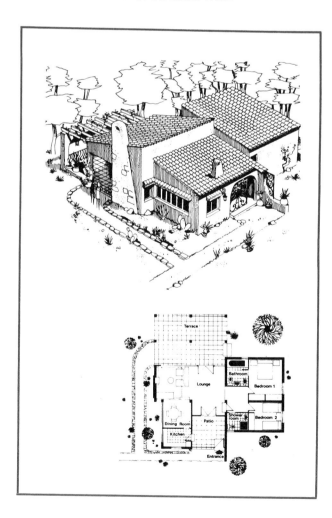

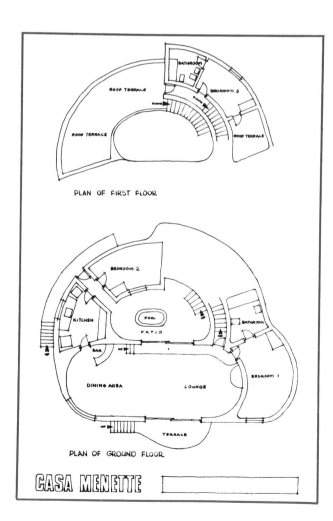

160, 161
*The old and the new in the Algarve, Portugal: the squat,
white cottage, left, has doorways surmounted by arches and
covings, and the chimneys are slender and elegant. Below, a
new village-style house at Vale do Lobo.
(Guide Michelin)*

122

162 (above)
The newly-built apartments Mar Azul at Praia da Oura near
Albufeira in Portugal.

163 (right)
These old, terraced cottages in South West France are in the
process of modernisation.
(Trevor Kenyon)

164 (above)
This small terraced house was originally part of the stables of the seventeenth-century château at Saussignac in South West France. Note the thickness of the walls where new windows are being fitted.
(Trevor Kenyon)

165 (below)
Over 1,000 acres on the north side of the island of Minorca are at present being developed by Tufnell Developers S.A. who plan to build a "fishermen's village" of 150 villas.

XXX (below)
The Minorcan farmhouse after its conversion, with white-washed walls and green shutters. The archways were designed by Denise Parsons, in keeping with the traditional Minorcan style, and built by a local builder.
(Nicholas Parsons)

166 (right)
Originally little more than a gap in the rocks with a handful of fishermen's cottages clustered round it, Binibeca in Minorca has now grown and has a village square with enchanting white-washed cottages connected by a maze of alleyways.

167 (below right)
A traditional harbour scene at Kyrenia, Cyprus.

168 (above)
The deeply arched terraces of the new building of Kyrenia
Castle Court follow the traditional style of architecture.

169 (below)
The drawings and plan show a cottage which is to be built in
the traditional style on the south-east coast of Elba.

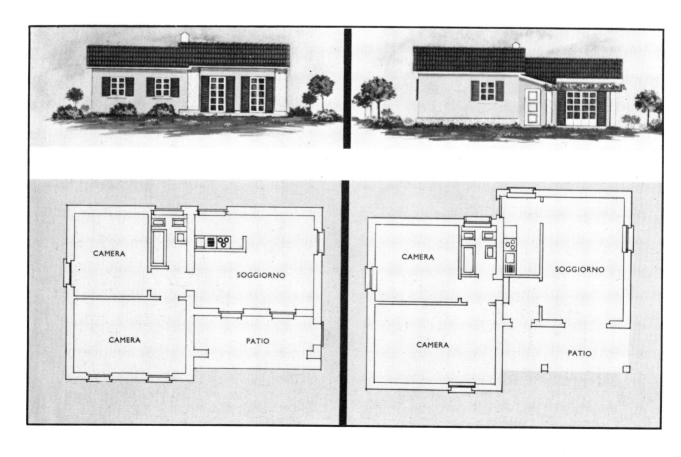

170 (above)
An old and traditional Swiss chalet in the mountains with its low-pitched eaves.
(Guide Michelin/Swiss National Tourist Office)

171 (below)
These chalets are part of a model village scheme called Anzère on a plâteau dominating the Rhône Valley in Canton Valais, Switzerland. The village is planned to contain chalets and apartments, hotels, pensions, restaurants, shops and small chalets known as mazots, *whose name is derived from the old small barns which were perched on piles and used as granaries or storehouses.*
(PRO – Anzère)

11
rehabilitating a ruin

The younger generation is not, it is said, like the old.
Lads go off to seek fortunes in towns, or cannot endure,
after the gaiety of barrack life, the monotony of the country.

The Pleasant Land of France (1908), ROWLAND E. PROTHERO

XXV
page 107

172

173, 174

175, 176,
177

178

The passion for doing up country property, whether it is a cottage, farmhouse, barn or water-mill, can be indulged in to complete satisfaction in the Dordogne area, that attractive history-packed part of South West France to the east of Bordeaux.

Derelict is not a dirty word in the Dordogne. A hole in the roof, or no roof at all, crumbling walls and no sanitation do not seem to deter the dedicated converter of the solid stone barns and dwellings originally used by French sons of the soil. Left to moulder away as the young went off to the cities to work, they are being sold off by local families to anyone who wants a country retreat; French, Americans and British are snapping them up, either for holiday use or retirement.

Barns are as much in demand in France for living in as they are in Britain. Thurloe Conolly, a British architect living in the Dordogne is an expert in their transformation. Show him a shell of a place, and in no time at all a roof is on, windows are fitted, floors tiled, and the whole thing is ready for occupation, simple holiday-style anyway.

One of the major attractions of "doing-up" in any part of the world also seems to be the "back-to-nature" syndrome – literally the creation of something with your own hands. I met John, a hotelier from Guernsey, who was, at the time, between businesses and having a well-earned rest(!) working with a local *maçon* (stonemason) and *charpentier* (carpenter), bringing new life to a magnificent barn *c.* 1775 near Saussignac. A large chicken house, family tomb, a couple of meadows and a wood were included in the "going for a song" price. It was pouring with rain when I went round the place, and I tramped ankle-deep in mud, but everyone was singing happily away as they worked in complete harmony!

There is an association in nearby Périgueux, capital of Périgord, which was set up to safeguard the conservation of these old country places.

They recommend that any restoration job should be in keeping with the traditional style of the area: the correct flat or canal tiles for the roof, not the new *mécanique* variety, stone for the walls quarried locally, windows with the right number of glazing bars, wood shutters and not metal, and no enlarging of dormer windows beyond their original opening.

If you wish to buy a building which has not been used for human habitation before, you should first obtain planning permission. The only people who are recognised for obtaining this permission are French architects, and it is a matter of law that one is employed for this type of work. The process of obtaining planning permission can be quite lengthy, but there is a professional organisation called the Bureau des Etudes in the larger towns, which can undertake all aspects of planning applications, building plans and supervision, and so on, in conjunction with the appropriately qualified French architects and builders.

With regard to buildings which have previously been used for human habitation – and this can be interpreted very loosely – it is not necessary to obtain any permission for the works required, except the following:

(a) Any out-of-character alterations to the exterior of the property are frowned upon both by the local inhabitants, and of course the preservation societies.

(b) For the sake of courtesy, the local mayor should be notified of the installation of a septic tank. In the majority of instances the mason who is installing the drains for you knows the Mayor personally, and will notify him accordingly.

Rural areas of France do not have a general builder who carries out all the work. You have to rely on independent, individual contractors who carry out individual trades, so it is necessary to employ probably four or five different tradesmen, and have a contract with each one.

The method of payment to the contractors is

usually one third at the start of the work, one third during the contract, and one third on completion. The standard of workmanship is good, but knowledge of the particular trades involved is extremely important. For example, it is possible to have a rough plaster internal finish carried out by a mason, which is approximately one third of the cost of a smooth plaster finish, which is carried out by a plasterer!

Local workers are there for the asking, but you have to be patient, remembering that each will be a miniature craftsman and must take his time. Also, as each trade works independently of the other, co-ordination and close supervision are essential.

A modest sum buys a small village house with a *cave* (a store room for wine barrels on the ground floor), a couple of large rooms, a *grenier* (attic) and a *grange* (barn) attached. But in many cases it will need everything, but *everything* done to it – a new roof, a floor to cover the existing rubble one, the building of interior walls to give living-room, bedrooms, kitchen, bathroom and lavatory and electricity and water will have to be brought in to provide the basics for cooking, lighting and sanitation.

The tricky problem of the loo will probably have to be solved by sinking a septic tank.

Remember that even a renovated house in reasonable condition, which could be complete with modern equipment such as cooker, refrigerator and television, may well have only a *petit coin* for essential purposes – an earth closet in a little hut at the bottom of the garden.

Shortage of water is a great problem in French country life. Mains water is limited and if you have a well, even one with an electric pump, and the water runs dry, there is nothing much you can do about it. Plenty of properties have mains electricity, but the problem here is that the whole wiring system is above ground. If there is a storm, the supply can be turned off without warning.

But if it is peace and tranquility, cool meadows and fertile plains, and the contrast of caverns and streams that you want to escape to, then the Dordogne is one of the loveliest and least spoilt areas of France. Read on for details of farmhouses to be converted in this area of rivers, châteaux and spectacular gorges . . .

172
Derelict is not a dirty word in the Dordogne. A hole in the roof or even no roof at all presents no problem – it can simply be re-timbered or re-tiled. This house is at present being given a new roof, new windows and a new floor. (Trevor Kenyon)

131

173
This early nineteenth-century barn in the Lot et Garonne valley in France was effectively restored from a ruin, with no roof and crumbling walls, into a holiday home.
(Thurloe Connolly)

174

The rebuilt roof was extended along the length of the
building to form a south-facing verandah with a low
retaining wall, below left, and all the main rooms open on to
this verandah. The front was completely restored, below
right, with new roof, windows and extension for bedrooms and
bathrooms. The impressive new living area, bottom left, is
45 feet (13·7 metres) long by 20 feet (6 metres) wide,
soaring to 20 feet (6 metres) high. New ceiling trusses have
been mixed in with the old beams and the room-divider is part
of the cattle stalls. The large window was made from the hay
loft opening. A central-heating radiator was fitted to the wall
near the window, bottom right, and the floor was later
covered with terracotta tiles.
(Thurloe Connolly)

175, 176, 177
This barn, built about 1775 near Saussignac in France, was recently bought for a "going for a song" price and is in the process of being brought back to life. The AV on the building above stands for A Vendre (for sale) and it is this main building only that is being used in the conversion. One of the first jobs was to fit windows in the side, left. Included in the price was a chicken house, two meadows, a wood and the family tomb, below left, complete with plastic flowers. (Trevor Kenyon)

178 (above)
This little old country cottage is typical of those in the
Périgord area of France with its lucarnes (dormer windows),
volets (shutters), and plat and canal tuiles (flat and canal
tiles). There is an association set up in Périgueux to
safeguard the conservation of these old country places.
(Fédération Nationale de Sauvegarde des Maisons et
Paysages de France)

179 (below)
A mélange of village house conversions in the Dordogne, with
flat, canal and the new mécanique tiles used for the roofs.
Note how closely packed together the houses are, as it was the
custom to terrace houses into the actual hillside.
(Trevor Kenyon)

12
farmhouses international

Un foyer sans feu. Une table sans pain. Une maison sans femme.

Old Breton Proverb

"A room without a fire, a table without bread, a house without a woman" is a very apt description of any of the old farmhouses left empty and decaying as the young go off to the cities to work and the spirit of the old houses withers away through disuse and neglect. Whether in Wales or in France, Sussex or Spain, the story is still very much the same. But now many of these simple farmhouses are gradually being brought back to life by the noise-stricken town-dweller anxious to enjoy the delights of country living.

The old farmhouses and hill cottages in Wales are so tucked away that they are almost impossible for a stranger to locate. The natives are helpful, but the old names have been out of circulation for so long, they have been forgotten.

Many of the dwellings have no access road, so you have to walk, or climb, over rough tracks. Searching for one described as "very peacefully and pleasantly situated in the heart of pastoral countryside off the main Aberystwyth/Cardigan road, with a pure, never-failing water supply and woodland to the rear", I drove round three villages, all the wrong ones, before finally finding the farmer to whom it belonged. So first find your farmer.

Directing me across a pot-hole pitted path around the back of his new house, "my" farmer pointed in the far distance and said the old farmhouse was over a bridge and behind the trees. Crossing the bridge, which was a narrow plank suspended precariously over rushing water, I kept going through soft, squelchy mud to find it. The place could well have been in France – no warmth, food or female had graced the place for many a year. Inside, there were partition walls of a kind, so thin that if you leant against them they would surely have fallen down. Up the rickety stairs, the little cell-like rooms under the eaves would just have taken a bed and no more.

Yet the thick, granite walls of the exterior were still solid, the wooden front door firm and stout (locked with an enormous key), so operation revival was clearly in order. New windows, new roof, proper internal walls and the more usual comforts of daily living would work wonders. Already many have been saved, some through the encouragement of the Welsh Cottage Property Advertiser which features this type of property through its newspaper, a publication almost entirely devoted to farm and other properties needing rehabilitation, as well as those already restored.

I lost my way in South West France too, driving around lanes just missing the stuffed-to-the-gills geese waddling around in preparation for their producing of foie-gras. I finally found my farmer, blue-bereted and apple-cheeked, who took me over Les Genêts, a small, 200-year-old, cement and stone walled farmhouse in a couple of acres. High grass nearly covered the entrance to the door, but the farmer told me: "Don't worry, my cows will eat all that in a morning". The place was bare inside and the outside rundown but it was still solid and could be repaired. The barn at the side of the house would convert to a kitchen and the stable on the other side of the living-room to a bathroom. The *grenier* (attic room) on the top still strung with the original wires on which tobacco was hung for drying, would just make two bedrooms.

With breathtaking views, a fig tree on the side wall, a cherry tree over the nearby oven, an inexhaustible well of drinking water, the use of an artificial lake with fish in it opposite and complete tranquility, what more could you want? All you need is the foresight, confidence, enterprise and initiative to see that the unwanted and forlorn can become desirable and delightful!

John Belsey, a chartered surveyor, and his wife, Elizabeth, live in an attractive, early nineteenth-century farmhouse, carefully restored, in Siorac de Ribérac, also in the Dordogne area of France. The house, overlooking a carp-filled pond and three acres of meadow, has thick, stone walls and a Roman tiled roof. The original beamed ceiling has been kept in the living area and the kitchen, main bedroom and bathroom have all been neatly fitted into the ground floor. Part of the enormous beamed loft over what was the granary has been converted into an extra bedroom which is used as a study.

If you want advice on restoration and repairs, surveys and valuations in the Dordogne, John

180

181

Belsey is one of the people to go to. "This kind of work interests me greatly as it enables me to make the best use of my experience in Britain as a building surveyor," he told me, but went on to warn: "However, I only work on a part-time basis, as I am much too interested in France and the French to spend all my time at a desk."

At Loubes-Bernac, Lot et Garonne, Ian and Madeline Williams's luxuriously converted farmhouse, La Charpentière, is a fabulous place, complete with minstrels' gallery, huge sitting-room with giant fireplace and antique working spit. The big master bedroom has a sunken bath and lavatory en suite, and there are three other double bedrooms plus another lavatory and shower. It is set in seven acres of garden and woodland and has an enormous patio and swimming pool.

Nicholas Parsons, leading television and stage personality, and his wife Denise, both of whom are well known on radio, bought an old farmhouse in the San Luis area of Minorca, on the South East of the island, which is the second largest and most easterly of the Balearics. San Luis was built during the French occupation between 1756 and 1763 to house Breton sailors. "We bought the farmhouse for a very low figure, and it didn't cost very much to convert it, because then everything was about three times cheaper than it is now," they told me. "We have done it very simply as we don't get the time to stay there as often as we would like. It is an uncomplicated conversion of a typical old Minorcan farmhouse."

Their neighbours are mixed nationalities, some Minorcan farmers, original inhabitants of the village, and other people, such as an actor, artist, businessman and writer, who like simple living and countrified property.

Nicholas's and Denise's farmhouse was very neglected and dilapidated when they bought it but, being of very solid structure, it was not beyond repair, even though it had not been lived in for some time. However, all the timbers had to be renewed, and new beams made on the first floor, although the roof beams were adequate. Windows were top priority too. A window was put in a top room which was turned into their bedroom. It had previously been a storage place under the roof, as is usual in this kind of Minorcan farm, so there were no windows in it originally. Other windows were either enlarged or replaced; in the bedrooms at the back tiny box-windows of typical local style were fitted.

In these old Minorcan farmhouses these rooms would have perhaps one little window high up so as not to let in too much cold in the winter or too much heat in the summer. The main bedroom at the back had a large window put in overlooking the road. For the kitchen window beside the door, a sash window was put in, as this is a typical Minorcan style inherited from the days of British occupation. The out-buildings were in a bad state of dilapidation and were rebuilt and made serviceable but not at this stage turned into somewhere to live. They found the local workmen were very good and quite artistic, with a great sense of design and a feeling for building.

Nicholas and Denise, both busy people, were unable to be there to oversee the work, so their agent, a Spanish woman, supervised it for them. It was reconstructed from pencil drawings that they left and, considering the problems experienced in rebuilding anywhere, the builders did a remarkable job. There were, of course, little mistakes and things sometimes turned out wrong, but on the whole they were very impressed with the work and the way the men did it.

Archways outside the house were designed by Denise in keeping with the Minorcan style, and they were built by the local builder from a pencil drawing. She explained: "There was nothing in the kitchen – we found the typical tiles and we designed the bar as a practical measure. The washing-up sink is one side and the serving area to the right. The food goes straight on the bar and it is attractive as well as practical. We now find that guests usually prefer to sit at the bar for drinks rather than go to the bigger living-room on the first floor."

XXIX
page 125
XXX
page 126

XXXI
page 143

There were, of course, many unforseen incidents – amusing and almost disastrous as well – during the progress of the work. The Parsons moved in and lived there for three weeks with the builders still working. One day the men were working on the roof and they dropped a tile right through the middle of the breakfast table – it could have killed somebody, but fortunately all it did was ruin a lovely and serviceable table!

When visitors stayed at the farmhouse, problems arose because the seepaway had not been built large enough. At first the Parsons had not intended to rent out the house, but as costs soared they soon realised it was essential. One large family followed another, none of whom had any experience of using equipment which was not on main drainage. Tenants used the large bathroom so much that it flooded the septic tank and, as it didn't seep away as it should have done, it naturally created a most unpleasant smell.

Nicholas recalls: "The builders came in the middle of the night to clean it out by hand and, although they promised to put the débris at the end of the garden, they left it spread across the field. It makes the soil marvellous for growing things, they explained. It is not surprising the friends who were renting the house at the time informed us they would like to find somewhere else to stay! Needless to say, we now have a large seepaway!"

XXXII
page 144

My friend Suzie, who has a Minorcan farmhouse, also in the San Luis area, had similar problems. She had to get permission to run electricity across other people's land, and the original sanitation was "just a smart little hut outside". Water was hauled up in a bucket from a well. More windows had to be put in too – one room in the centre of the farmhouse was completely dark. The décor has been kept simple: white paint everywhere, even on the beams, and the original red-tiled floors have been polished up, with rush matting used where appropriate. Interesting innovations include canal-type roof tiles used as wall-lights, and wall-seats built of stone and topped with bright cushions covered with deckchair canvas.

On the Costa Blanca in Spain, many of the old farmhouses have already been snapped up for conversion. My first discovery was a tiny one-storey *caseta* (virtually a little hut), probably 150 years old, at the back of Javea, with views of the mountains. It was very simple, with a tiled floor, and had recently been in use. The basic, yet adequate, furnishings were still there – low, cane chairs, a rough wood table, and simple pots and pans. Behind a thin board partition at the side of the room was an ancient iron bedstead.

188

It had been bought through Overseas Sales Organisation, and designer Christopher Simmons was at work on a full-scale conversion. With another piece built on the back to provide three bedrooms each with its own bathroom, the little hut would eventually become quite a grand house.

189

Nearby was a farmhouse that had been modernised and, although a larger structure, the basic shape of the other smaller one was there. The archways on to the terrace, the beamed main room, the fireplace and the tiled floor were all in the same style as the little *caseta*. It was almost like seeing an instant conversion.

190

191

Farm property in Portugal is strong and sturdy. One old farmhouse in the Algarve, 19 kilometres from Faro, was awaiting conversion when I heard of it through the agents, Tufnell International. It was built of stone, with very thick solid walls, completely dry, and well roofed with the original Algarve tiles. There were six rooms on the ground floor, and one room upstairs leading on to a terrace from which could be seen marvellous views of the countryside and part of the coastline, as well as the mountains of Monchique in the distance. The Sierra Monchique is a volcanic block rising more than 2,000 feet (600 metres) high. The soil is rich and the land is planted abundantly with olive, fig, almond, pear, orange and lemon trees, and numerous vines.

On one end of the house was a large cowshed, with forage store above, which could without difficulty be incorporated into the main house. In addition there were several other out-buildings which could be used as garage, workshops, studios or guest cottages. Water was in a large cistern which caught the rainwater, and a generator was needed for electricity and to pump the water into the house.

"Alone on their mounds, old farms are ennobled by the fine shapes of pines or cypresses, standing out against a pale blue sky." So goes the description of the beautiful Tuscan countryside in the Michelin Green Guide to Italy.

I have picked out two Italian farmhouses in Tuscany to illustrate. One is ready for restoration, the other has already been transformed. I feel I cannot improve on the delightful fact sheets I was sent from Italy about them, all translated in the inimitable Latin style. They are reproduced exactly as they were given to me.

LE CACCIAIE

Type: old and typical farm-house.
Zone: in the Chianti Classico, 3 minutes from the village Gaiole, 25 km from Siena, 45 km from Florence, 15 km from the motor-way "del Sole" (Montevarchi).
Access: excellent, for every vehicle.
Position: on a small table-land, dominating a lovely brook, on the slope of a green Chianti-valley. Beautiful, country-like view on the near vine-yards, woods and meadows. Altitude: 400 m.
Seclusion: just right, neighbours at 300/400 m.
State: very strong farm-house, in excellent state of conservation.
Description: classical style of farm-house with an elevated dove-cot. Roof with four sides. A vaulted staircase brings you up to the first floor in a large kitchen with a fire-place. 6/7 other rooms are happily placed around it. From the kitchen an old wooden staircase is getting up to the dove-cot. On the ground-floor there are the old stables which can be easily adapted – without great expense – in dwelling-rooms.

Water/Electricity: Water is abounding (well in the yard). Electricity is installed.

Dependencies: several and large ones, among them a beautiful barn – easily to be adapted.

Estate: 1,5 Ha is surrounding the farm-house. There are some vine-trees, meadows and so on.

Restoring-works: Everything is well conserved, the restoring-works could be limited on the installation of bath-rooms, WC, kitchen-angle and the normal cleaning-works and putting in order.

Conclusion: It is a really interesting object. Beautiful position, immediately to be inhabited with a few expenses, very typical house which shall be a pleasant and sure dwelling-place.

STELLA

Type: old farm, perfectly restored.

Zone: Under the city-wall of San Gimignano, 1 km from the gates of the town.

Position: dominating, with a remarkable panorama that goes as far as the hills of the Chianti.

Access: good public road, a little steepy.

Isolation: absolute tranquility 3 minutes from San Gimignano.

State: restored 2 years ago, the house is in perfect state.

Description: Rectangular construction (14 × 8 m). On the ground-floor there are a bed-room with bath/toilet, the kitchen, the laundry, a big living-room with chimney, a small lobby, a a bath/toilet. You reach the first floor either by a beautiful external stair or by a small internal stair. There are a living-room with chimney, 3 bed-rooms and 2 bathrooms (with ceramique and so on). The whole arrangement is made with a lot of taste and without saving of means. There is central heating, boilers, electric and gas.

Water: Public pipeline.

Electricity: installed.

Estate: about 5,000 m2 (fenced).

Dependencies: a terrace with pergola on the back of the house, a fine barn.

Available: The house is still occupied by its owner who asks for a notice of 3 or 4 month in case of no other agreement.

Note: The house is furnished. The furniture (of taste and value) is not included in the price. In case of any interest, the purchase of the furniture can be done separately.

Conclusion: A delicious dwelling-place that has been arranged with a remarkable taste and is available immediately, without any costs. The position is characterised by its tranquillity, its marvellous view at the gates of the medieval town of San Gimignano.

180 (top)
Many simple farmhouses are gradually being brought back to life – this simple house in Sussex, about 200 years old, has been skilfully restored.
(Trevor Kenyon)

181 (centre)
No warmth, food or female had graced this old farmhouse in Wales for many years. But with its solid granite walls and stout front door it was ripe for conversion.
(Trevor Kenyon)

182 (above)
Already many properties in Wales have been saved – this one has been given a new roof, new windows and a coat of paint.
(The Welsh Cottage Property Advertiser, Aberystwyth)

139

183 (below)
Les Genêts, a small, 200-year-old farmhouse I visited in the Dordogne district of France, needed complete restoration. High grass hid the entrance but the farmer assured me that his cows would eat it in a morning. The cement and stone walled exterior was solid but the interior was primitive with an earth floor, no damp-proof course and no services.
(Trevor Kenyon)

184 (right)
This forlorn farmhouse in the Dordogne needs plenty of loving care and attention to bring it back to life.
(Trevor Kenyon)

185 (below right)
A more desirable property was this delightful farmhouse near Périgueux in the Dordogne. The bottom floor is slightly below ground level and contains the cave for the wine store or stables. The outside stone steps lead to the first-floor living rooms to bypass any animals down below.

140

186, 187
La Charpentière at Loubes-Bernac in Lot et Garonne, France, is a luxuriously converted farmhouse and barn which includes a vast patio and swimming pool, above, and seven acres of garden and woodland. The interior of the barn has been made into a long living-room, below, with a minstrels' galley on the right of the picture which, together with a great deal of the furniture, was made by local French craftsmen. On the left is a large fireplace with an antique working spit. (Trevor Kenyon)

XXXI
*The kitchen and serving area in the Parsons' converted
farmhouse has been decorated in typical Minorcan style with
white walls, large patterned tiles on one of the walls and
on the bar, and plain orange tiles on the top of the bar.*

XXXII
Another typical farmhouse in the San Luis area of Minorca which was bought for conversion. Like the Parsons' house it had very few windows and one of the rooms was completely dark.

188
This tiny caseta – little more than a hut – near Javea on the Costa Blanca in Spain is one of many that are being bought up quickly for conversion. It consists basically of one large room with a door to a partitioned-off area on the right used for sleeping quarters. The floor is tiled and the ceiling beamed, and there is a fireplace on the left. After modernisation, there will be three bedrooms, each with its own bathroom, built on to the back.
(Trevor Kenyon)

189, 190
Although a much larger building than the tiny caseta on the Costa Blanca, this newly modernised farmhouse nearby has the basic shape, above. Even the interior, left, with its fireplace, beamed ceiling and tiled floor, is very similar, although much grander in style.
(Trevor Kenyon)

191 (top right)
This is a typical Portuguese farmhouse in the Algarve. On the ground floor are the stables, wine and other store-rooms, and the living accommodation on the first floor is reached by the outside flight of stone steps leading on to a terrace.
(Guide Michelin)

192 (right)
Le Cacciaie in the Chianti Classico district of Italy, an old and typical farmhouse with an elevated dovecot, awaits modernisation. On the ground floor are the old stables and on the first floor, reached by a vaulted staircase, is the living accommodation.

193
Stella, a restored farmhouse in San Gimignano, Italy, is described on the fact sheet as "a delicious dwelling-place in perfect state. The position is characterised by its tranquillity" and it is approached by "a good public road, a little steepy". At the back of the house is a terrace with pergola and a fine barn.

194
The arrangement of the interior of Stella is described on the fact sheet as being "made with a lot of taste and without saving of means".

13
converting the rock

In Xanadu did Kubla Khan
A stately pleasure-dome decree . . .

And 'mid these dancing rocks at once and ever
It flung up momently the sacred river . . .

The shadow of the dome of pleasure
Floated midway on the waves;
Where was heard the mingled measure
From the fountain and the caves . . .

For he on honey-dew hath fed,
And drunk the milk of Paradise.

Kubla Khan, SAMUEL TAYLOR COLERIDGE

The printed details of La Manzanera, the pop-fantasy village hewn out of the rock on the Costa Blanca in Spain, open with the refrain from The Trip by Jimi Hendrix. But the haunting words of Samuel Taylor Coleridge in Kubla Khan, are just as appropriate when describing the exciting buildings that go to make up this amazing rocky complex.

The pagoda-shaped apartment block, an olive-green building with a fortress-like quality, is appropriately christened Xanadu, and a veritable pleasure-dome it is. Converted from the rocky slopes by the fishing village of Calpe, its shape follows the spirit of the Peñón de Ifach a huge rock on a peninsula protecting the harbour. The architect is Ricardo Bofill, a brilliant "new wave" Spanish designer following in the style of Barcelona's great Antoni Gaudi of *Sagrada Familia* fame.

The design of Xanadu, almost assymetrical, is claimed as a prototype experiment of a garden city in space. Each apartment is made up of any three cubes selected from a choice of living, sleeping and service units. Shaded internal terraces are cool and quiet. The central stairwell of stone steps is broken up by circular openings which give a sort of bird's eye view of each passage. It is not hard to imagine "the mingled measure from the fountain and the caves" echoing in "the shadow of the dome of pleasure".

Whether it will retain its milk-of-paradise air remains to be seen. It has taken seven years to build 60 units and it will take another six years to complete the whole concept, for La Manzanera will also include castle-like bungalows, El Castillo, and villas made out of rock.

Another apartment block that has been completed in La Manzanera is Muralla Roja (Red Wall), which has 52 apartments. El Castillo Rojo, as it is also called, is strangely aggressive. The architecture has strong vertical lines, reminiscent of the "hard-edge" look of the 1920s.

On the inside looking out it's fine, but as I approached the exterior, blood-red against the gentle blue sky, I found it soul-destroying. You need to be tough to take the square blocks and the almost cell-like appearance of the building and, as the developers point out: "Tolerance, international thinking and intellectual interests are a must for the interested purchaser". They claim that the interior has been designed to be both modern and rational, without unnecessary details or wasted space.

"The architect likes to think of the entire apartment as an enormous bed with thinking, eating, drinking and enjoyment corners." This is part of the overall concept "where today's world is not the one of yesterday but rather of tomorrow".

An unusual conversion from the rock is La Aguilera, the Eagle's Nest, built against the sloping face of the craggy cliffs of the rocky promontory Espejo del Mar, the mirror of the sea. It is above the beach of Bahia La Parra, five miles west of Almeria in the district of Andalucia, Costa del Sol.

197

198

Each storey is stepped back up the rock face, a masterpiece of structural engineering, steel-framed and with brick cavity wall construction. You enter from the top of the promontory where lifts take you down from a marble-lined entrance to the 14 storeys below. The apartments are of duplex design, that is, occupying split levels, with an internal staircase connecting the entry floor to the terrace floor below – almost a villa within a block.

Hailed as the most original architectural triumph around the Mediterranean basin in France, is Jacques Couelle's Port La Galère, with its cluster of houses built up from the red rocks of the Midi. It is a village about eight miles west of Cannes, achieving a remarkable degree of organic unity with the rocky landscape. The sculptured arcades with their deeply curved archways, terraces, balconies and galleries are of concrete block construction.

Dramatic organic architecture pops up again in the Aga Khan's luxury development of the Costa Smeralda in Sardinia. Jacques Couelle was responsible for the first phase and his son, Savin, is continuing the skilful and imaginative conversion of the rocky sites in Porto Cervo.

Building regulations stipulate that the land should not be spoiled by towering multistoreyed blocks, and that the elevation of any

houses should not ruin the natural contours of the land. So, no rocks or trees are removed when building a house, and the natural rocks become incorporated into its design. Some houses have "natural rooms" outside in a courtyard, their shapes formed by the shapes of rocks and trees.

Doorways are fitted into natural curves of the rocks and windows are just glazed shapes inset into the rocky walls. Great lumps of rock, mosaic-covered, form a table, openings in the rock form a fireplace and steps for a staircase are hewn into the rock and tiled.

Another spectacular architect is Michel Busiri Vici. His work, too, blends harmoniously with the rocky landscape. A long, low, single-storey villa, one of the most impressive, privately-owned dwellings on the Costa Smeralda, has the whole of its enormous flat roof as a sun terrace.

195

Xanadu, an olive-green, pagoda-shaped apartment block, part of the La Manzanera complex, has been converted from the rocky slopes by the fishing village of Calpe on the Costa Blanca in Spain. Claimed as a prototype experiment of a garden city in space, its shape follows the spirit of the Peñón de Ifach, a huge rock on a peninsula protecting the harbour. (Trevor Kenyon)

199

200

196 (above)
Each apartment in Xanadu is made up of any three cubes
selected from a choice of living, sleeping and service units,
with a shaded, internal terrace, on the right of the picture. The
tiles are built up to form seating areas, with cushions on the
top, and in the main bedroom a vast sunken area is tiled to
form the sleeping area. Through the archway is the dining area
and beyond that the kitchen.
(Trevor Kenyon)

197 (below)
Muralla Roja (Red Wall) is another apartment block that has
been completed in the La Manzanera complex near Calpe.
The square blocks and almost cell-like appearance of the
building, together with its blood-red walls, give it a rather
aggressive air, but the developers claim that it has been
designed to be both modern and rational without any
unnecessary details or wasted space.
(Trevor Kenyon)

198, 199
La Aguilera, the Eagle's Nest, left, is an apartment block converted from the rock. This one is built against the sloping face of the cliffs above the beach of Bahia La Parra near Almeria in Spain. Each storey is stepped back up the rock face and you enter from the top of the building and travel by lift to the 14 storeys below. Each apartment occupies split levels, below, so that they are almost like separate villas. An internal staircase connects the entry floor, comprising bedroom and bathroom, with the terrace floor below, consisting of a kitchen, living-room and patio.
(Sovrensa, Almeria, Spain)

200 (right)
Deep balcony-terraces dominate the external appearance of these concrete houses built in the red rocks on the Mediterranean, near Cannes. Called Port La Galère, the village achieves remarkable unity with the rocky landscape.
(Cement and Concrete Association)

152

201
Building regulations for the Aga Khan's luxury development
at Porto Cervo in Sardinia stipulate that the elevation of
houses should not spoil the natural contours of the land, so
all the rocks and trees have become incorporated into the
design. The interior of the house, below, looks as though it has
grown naturally from its rocky surroundings into a
sophisticated design for living. The mosaic-covered lump of
rock at the end of the steps forms a table, and boulder-like
stones surround the open fireplace. The ceiling, wood-beamed
interspersed with bamboo, completes the natural look.
(The Costa Smeralda Information Office)

202
Another architect whose work blends well into the
surrounding landscape is Michel Busiri Vici. One of the most
impressive, privately owned villas on the Costa Smeralda in
Sardinia is this one, set against a mountainous backdrop,
with the whole of its flat roof designed as a sun terrace.
(The Costa Smeralda Information Office)

acknowledgments

Colour photographs

I

The Wedge, Windlesham, Surrey
Owner: Bettie Spurling
Exterior is painted with ICI Dulux
Weathershield Brilliant White, Dulux
Wedgwood Blue, and Dulux Black
Gloss

III

Exterior of cottage is painted with ICI
Dulux Weathershield Paint

V, VI, IX

Regency House, West Sussex
Sitting-room: walls and ceiling are
covered with ICI hessian. Loose covers
on the chairs are made of Sanderson
hessian-type fabric, and the print over
the mantelpiece is edged with Sanderson
silk
Attic bedroom: ICI Yarna textured
wallcovering on walls and units. The
Liden whitewood chest-of-drawers unit
is also painted with Crown Plus Two
Brilliant White
Decorator: Alec Menday
Renovation work: Hickie and Lewis

XII, XIII, XIV

The Barn, Sussex
Kitchen: yellow Polycell mosaic tiles
surround the kitchen sink. Surfaces are
painted with Crown Plus Two
Polyurethane gloss paint
Bedsitting-room: walls are painted with
Durotex; fabrics for curtains, chairs and
divan by Sanderson
Exterior: garage and hoist doors are
painted with Crown Seagull Gloss, and
the front door with Hadrian Geranium
Gloss
Roof: Turnerised Roofing Co. (Gt.
Britain) Ltd., London

XVI, XVII, XVIII, XIX, XX, XXI
Weald House, Pluckley, Kent
Owner and conversion ideas: Michael
Brandt

XV

**The Old Barn, Carperby,
Wensleydale**
Project of Your Cottage in the Country
Ltd., York

XXII, XXIII
Roma Jay's former kitchen
Conversion: Jay Kitchen Consultants,
London
Window blinds by Nairn

XXIV
**The Dower House, Old Windsor,
Berkshire**
Owner: Major Timothy Tufnell MC
Interior decoration: Colin Stone
Art-nouveau design wallpaper by
Sanderson

XXVI
**Peyduré, 24 Siorac de Ribérac,
Dordogne, France**
Owner and surveyor: H. J. Belsey
FRICS
Agent: Burton and Evans, London

Black and white photographs

9, 10, 11
Timber decay specialists: Richardson and
Starling Ltd., Winchester, Hants.

12
**Cherrytree Cottage, near Midhurst,
Sussex**
Agent: King and Chasemore,
Pulborough, Sussex

14
Skitreadons, Haslemere, Surrey
Agent: Harrods Estate Offices,
Haslemere, Surrey

18
Beach Cottage, Worthing, Sussex
Builders: Edw. Snewin

19
Cottage in Worthing, Sussex
Agent: Mitchell and Co., Worthing,
Sussex

20
The Brewers Cottage, Denbighshire
Agent: Jackson-Stops and Staff, Chester,
Cheshire

21
**Farm cottage in the Dordogne,
France**
Agent: Keith Wilson, Berbiguières,
Dordogne, France

22
**Pokabaig, Skye, Inverness-shire,
Scotland**
Owner: Lucy Grant
Exterior is painted with Dulux
Weathershield Brilliant White

30
Shaston Way, Wiltshire
Aquaseal products from Berry Wiggins,
Rochester, Kent

32
**Freefolk Cottage, Bletchley,
Buckinghamshire**
Heating is by a Majorca Glow-Worm
gas fire back boiler

33, 34, 35
**Meadow Cottage, Wyboston,
Bedfordshire**
Architect: Victor J. F. Farrar RIBA,
Bedford
Exterior is painted with Sandtex

36, 37, 38, 39
**Merrythought Cottage, Thriplow,
Royston, Hertfordshire**
Owner: Ashley Larmuth

41
The Wedge, Windlesham, Surrey
Owner: Bettie Spurling
Exterior is painted with ICI Dulux
Weathershield Brilliant White.
Shutters, window frames, front door,
gutterings and flower barrel are painted
with Dulux Wedgwood Blue, and
wrought-iron cottage name plate and
porch painted with Dulux Black Gloss

42, 43, 44
Farm Cottage, Dorset
Original conversion: Ashley Larmuth

45, 46, 47, 49, 50, 51, 55
Regency House, West Sussex
Exterior brickwork is painted with
Crown Stronghold Masonry Paint;
woodwork with Hadrian Black Gloss
and front door with Hadrian Geranium
Gloss
General restoration: D. H. Amey
Rear balcony, architect: A. S. Kemp
LRIBA
Rear balcony, builders: Edw. Snewin
All walls in garden apartment are painted
with Crown Brilliant White emulsion;
curtains and covers by Sanderson

62, 63, 64, 65
King's Barn, Berkshire
Architect: Dr. Irena Mardi, London

66, 67
**Rudge Hall, Rudge, near Frome,
Somerset**
Conversion: Viscountess Long of
Wraxhall, through her country
conversion company, Long Estates,
Steeple Ashton Manor, near Trowbridge,
Wiltshire
Agents: Bernard Thorpe and Partners,
Bath and Pearsons, Trowbridge,
Wiltshire

68, 69, 70
**Tithe Barn, Tredington,
Warwickshire**
Agent: Jackson-Stops and Staff, Chester,
Cheshire

71, 72
**The Barn, Collingham,
Nottinghamshire**
Owner: Geoffrey Bray
Building conversion: W. A. J. Russell,
Collingham, Nottinghamshire.
The house is heated by means of a
floor-standing Potterton gas
central-heating boiler in the kitchen
which supplies 12 radiators and provides
domestic hot water

73
**Grange Barn, Haversham, near
Wolverton, Buckinghamshire**
Agent: Connells, Bletchley,
Buckinghamshire

75, 76
**The Old Barn, Carperby,
Wensleydale**
Conversion: Your Cottage in the
Country Ltd., York
Architects: Gill Dockray Rhodes and
Moore, Kendal, Westmorland

77, 78, 79
**The Old Barn, West Witton,
Wensleydale**
Conversion: Your Cottage in the
Country Ltd., York
Architects: Gill Dockray Rhodes and
Moore, Kendal, Westmorland

80, 81
Starbotton Barn, Yorkshire
Conversion: Your Cottage in the
Country Ltd., York
Architects: James Hartley and Son
ARIBA

82, 83, 84, 85, 86
House in Hampstead, London
Conversion: Roomaloft Ascot
Rooflight window by Velux
Art-nouveau style wallpaper by
Sanderson

87, 88, 89, 90, 91
House in Finchley, London
Conversion: Roomaloft Ascot

92, 93
Roma Jay's former kitchen
Conversion: Jay Kitchen Consultants,
London

94, 95, 96
54 Meadway, Southgate, London
Owners: Tony and Roma Jay
Conversion: Jay Kitchen Consultants,
London
The kitchen contains a Pland one and a
half sink unit with a Whisk-o-matic
waste disposal unit in the half sink,
a 12-place AEG dishwasher, Scholtes
cooking hob with Moulinex Rotisserie
and grill over. Kenneth Clark's dark
brown and orange tiles are on the wall
and the work surfaces are covered
with Arborite Tru Copper with a
Cirrus design. Flooring is Armstrong's
orange, pink and mauve vinyl, and
Sandersons vinyl paper is used on walls,
ceiling and pelmets. The curved bench
seat in the eating area is covered with
Nairn geranium vinyl

97, 98
Kiln Cottage, Kent
Conversion: Jay Kitchen Consultants,
London

99, 100, 101
Conversion: Jay Kitchen Consultants,
London
The kitchen contains a Hygena unit of
double sink with cupboards above, a
Moffat split-level cooker, Scholtes hob,
Bendix washing machine and UPO
refrigerator

102
Conversion: Jay Kitchen Consultants,
London

103
Campton Manor, Bedfordshire
Agent: Knight, Frank and Rutley,
London

104
Daintrey House, Petworth, Sussex
Agent: King and Chasemore,
Pulborough, Sussex

105, 106
**The Manor House, Toot Baldon,
near Oxford**
Agent: Peter Gilbert Associates
(Country Properties) Ltd., Oxford
Conversion: Butterfield Gilbert Country
Properties Ltd., Maidenhead
Contractors: Phipps and Wynn
(Oxford) Ltd.
Design and control: Peter Gilbert
Decoration: Freda Gilbert

109
Asgill House, Richmond, Surrey
Owner: Fred Hauptfuhrer
Architect: Donald Insall FRIBA

111
The Dower House, Old Windsor, Berkshire
Owner: Major Timothy Tufnell MC

114
The Logs, Hampstead, London
Architect: Alexander Gibson ARIBA
The Conversion of Old Buildings into New Houses, C. Bernard Brown, Batsford 1955

119, 120, 121, 122, 123, 124, 125
Coach House, Essex
Owner: Rosemary Borland
Architect: John Amor ARIBA, Chipping Ongar, Essex
Builder: T. and E. Dellar of S. A. Mills, Kelvedon Hatch, Essex
Interior décor by Rosemary Borland

126, 127
Tower House, Park Village West, London
Architect: Scarlett Burkett Associates, London

128, 129, 130
De Vere Mews, Kensington, London
Agent: Barlow Cannon Estates Ltd., London
Architects: Triad, London
Contractors and Developers: Griffin Mellors and Associates, Birmingham
Project Manager: Bryan Griffin

131, 132, 133, 134
Pym Gate House, Cheshire
Original conversion: Ashley Larmuth

135, 136, 137
The Coach House, Courtwick Park, near Littlehampton, Sussex
Owner: Aileen Trump
Agent: King and Chasemore Building Design Department, Pulborough, Sussex

138
Moulin de Vesignol, Périgord, France
Agent: A. Dauta, Bergerac and Cabinet Marty-Crassat, Ribérac, France

139
Low Mill, Grassington, Wharfedale, Yorkshire
Conversion: Your Cottage in the Country Ltd., York

140
Littleborne Water Mill, Canterbury, Kent
Agent: Amos and Dawton, Canterbury
Builder: A. Hodgetts, Canterbury

141, 142
Bleadney Mill, Somerset
Owner: Leonard Taylor

143
Bassingbourn Mill, Hertfordshire
Agent: Knight, Frank and Rutley, London

144
Sawmill, Kerry, Montgomeryshire
Agent: Morris, Marshall and Poole, Newtown, Montgomeryshire

147, 148
Saltings, Egloshayle, Wadebridge, Cornwall
Owner: Arthur and Barbara Dongray
Architect: Roy W. Sale ARIBA, Cornwall
Contractor: J. Tucker, Wadebridge, Cornwall

149, 150, 151, 152
Whistling Green, Crayke, near Easingwold, York
Conversion: Your Cottage in the Country Ltd., York
Architect: Michael Butterworth ARIBA

156
Villa in El Tosalet, Javea, Spain
Agent: OSO S.A., London

157
Villa at Finca Campello, near Alicante, Spain
Agent: Owners Services Ltd., London, and Broxbourne, Hertfordshire

158
Casa Menette, near Moraira, Spain
Agent: Chilcott, White and Co., Croydon, Surrey

159
Cuarton, near Algeciras, Spain
Agent: Tufnell International, London

161
Village-style house at Vale do Lobo, Algarve, Portugal
Agent: Knight, Frank and Rutley, London

162
Apartments Mar Azul, Praia da Oura, near Albufeira, Algarve, Portugal
Agent: Tufnell International, London

166
Binibeca, Minorca, Spain
Agent: Binibella Ltd., London

168
Kyrenia Castle Court, Kyrenia, Cyprus
Agent: Sunvil International Sales Ltd., London

169
Cottage, Ortano Mare, Elba
Agent: Knight, Frank and Rutley,
London

171
Anzère, Canton Valais, Switzerland
Agent: Knight, Frank and Rutley,
London

172
House in the Dordogne, France
Agent: Keith Wilson, Berbiguières,
Dordogne, France, and Nicholas
Brimblecombe, South Cave, Brough,
E. Yorks

173, 174
Barn in Lot et Garonne, France
Designer: Thurloe Conolly, Lacapelle
Cabanac, South West France

175, 176, 177
Barn near Saussignac, France
Agent: Ian and Madeline Williams,
Loubes-Bernac 47, Lot et Garonne,
France

180
**Milliards Manor Farmhouse,
Westergate, Sussex**
Original conversion and former
owner: John Batten

181
Farmhouse in Wales
Agent: Evans Brothers, Aberaeron,
Cardiganshire

183
Les Genêts, Dordogne, France
Agent: European Property Services,
London and Leonce Varaillon, Ribérac,
France

184
Farmhouse in the Dordogne, France
Agent: Carter Associates, Sevenoaks,
Kent

185
**Farmhouse near Périgueux,
Dordogne, France**
Agent: Knight, Frank and Rutley,
London, and Cabinet Marty-Crassat,
Ribérac, France

186, 187
**La Charpentière, Loubes-Bernac 47,
Lot et Garonne, France**
Owners: Ian and Madeline Williams

188
**Caseta, near Javea, Costa Blanca,
Spain**
Agent: OSO S.A., London
Designer: Christopher Simmons

189, 190
**Farmhouse near Javea, Costa Blanca,
Spain**
Occupier: David Young
Agent: OSO S.A., London

192
**Le Cacciaie, near Gaiole, Chianti
Classico, Italy**
Agent: Knight, Frank and Rutley,
London

193, 194
Stella, San Gimignano, Italy
Agent: Knight, Frank and Rutley,
London

195, 196
**Xanadu, La Manzanera, Calpe,
Costa Blanca, Spain**
Occupier at time of photographs:
Oliver Kelly
Agent: International Services Ltd.,
London. (The former representative was
Oliver Kelly who now, with Michael
Smith, runs Interstate Realty, London,
and Benidorm, Spain. This is the
marketing organisation for Temoin
S.A., a property development, headed
by Luis Arriola Vignier, whose new
developments are Benidorm Springs,
Alahama Springs and Sierra de Altea)
Architect: Ricardo Bofill

197
**Muralla Roja, La Manzanera, Calpe,
Costa Blanca, Spain**
Agent: International Services Ltd.,
London
Architect: Ricardo Bofill

198, 199
**La Aguilera, Espejo del Mar,
Almeria, Costa del Sol, Spain**
Agents: Sovereign Southern S.A.,
Spain, and First St. George's Investment
Trust Ltd., London

200
Port La Galère, near Cannes, France
Architect: Jacques Couelle

201
**House in Porto Cervo, Costa
Smeralda, Sardinia**
Architect: Savin Couelle

202
Villa, Costa Smeralda, Sardinia
Architect: Michael Busiri Vici

If you have any cottage and conversion
ideas, the author, June Field, would be
interested to hear from you. Write c/o
John Bartholomew & Son Ltd. at
216 High Street, Bromley BR1 1PW

159

bibliography

CONVERSIONS

AS GOOD AS NEW, A GUIDE TO THE CONVERSION OF OLD PROPERTY, *Macfarlane Widdup*, Elek Books 1971

CONVERTING A COTTAGE, *Suzanne Beedell*, Sphere Books 1968

CONSERVATION OF BUILDINGS, *John Harvey*, John Baker 1972

COUNTRY COTTAGE CONVERTING CODE, The London Property Letter, Stonehart Publications 1972

DOING UP A HOUSE, *Mary Gilliatt*, Bodley Head 1968

HOUSE CONVERSION FOR EVERYONE, *Gladys Williams*, Robert Hale 1966

HOUSE AND GARDEN BOOK OF COTTAGES, *Joyce Lowrie ARIBA*, Collins/Condé Nast 1970

THE CONVERSION OF OLD BUILDINGS INTO NEW HOUSES FOR OCCUPATION AND INVESTMENT, *C. Bernard Brown*, Batsford 1955

THE THATCHER'S CRAFT, Rural Industries Bureau 1961

THE WELSH COTTAGE PROPERTY ADVERTISER, Aberystwyth

YOUR COUNTRY COTTAGE, *R. C. Edmunds*, David & Charles 1970

YOUR HOLIDAY HOME, *Audrey Powell,* David & Charles 1972

LOOKING FOR AND CHOOSING A HOUSE, Property Assessment Publications 1972

THE HOUSE YOU INTEND TO BUY, Property Assessment Publications 1972

HOME EXTENSIONS

BUILD YOUR OWN HOME EXTENSION, *H. F. Cochrane LRIBA*, John Gifford 1969

EXTENDING YOUR HOUSE, *edited by Edith Rudinger*, Consumers' Association 1971

HOUSES AND THEIR HISTORY

A HISTORY OF THE ENGLISH HOUSE, *N. Lloyd*, Architectural Press 1931

ENGLISH COTTAGES AND FARMHOUSES, *Olive Cook and Edwin Smith*, Thames & Hudson 1960

ENGLISH HOUSES, *Doreen Yarwood*, Batsford 1966

ENGLISH VILLAGE HOMES AND COUNTRY BUILDINGS, *Sydney Jones*, Batsford 1947

HOUSES IN THE COUNTRY, *Peter Gresswell*, Batsford 1964

OLD ENGLISH COUNTRY COTTAGES, *edited by Charles Holme,* The Studio 1906

OLD ENGLISH HOUSES, *Hugh Braun*, Faber & Faber 1962

THE ENGLISH COTTAGE, *H. Batsford and C. Fry*, Batsford 1950

THE ENGLISH FARMHOUSE, *M. S. Briggs*, Batsford 1953

THE FAMILY HOUSE IN ENGLAND, *Andrew Henderson*, Phoenix House 1964

THE HOUSE AND HOME, *M.W. Barley,* Vista Books 1963

THE MEDIEVAL HOUSE, *M. E. Wood,* 1965

THE PATTERN OF ENGLISH BUILDING, *Alec Clifton-Tayler*, Faber 1972

THE SMALLER ENGLISH HOUSE 1500–1939, *R. Turnor*, Batsford 1952

THE TIMBER-FRAME HOUSE IN ENGLAND, *Trudy West*, David & Charles 1971

THE TRUTH ABOUT COTTAGES, *John Woodforde*, Routledge & Kegan Paul 1969

THE WELSH HOUSE, *I. C. Peate*, Brython Press 1940

THIS OLD HOUSE, *David Iredale,* Shire Publications

TIMBER BUILDING IN ENGLAND FROM EARLY TIMES TO THE END OF THE 17TH CENTURY, *F. H. Crossley*, Batsford 1951

OVERSEAS PROPERTY

EARLY HOUSES OF OHIO, *I. T. Frary,* Constable: Dover Publications, New York 1970

GUIDE DES VILLAGES ABANDONNES, *Robert Landry,* Henri Balland, Hatchette 1970

LES MAISONS DE CAMPAGNE ETAIENT DES FERMES, *introduction par G. and M. Moguilensky ,* éditions Charles Massin, Paris

OVERSEAS PROPERTY GUIDE, *Arthur Bowers,* Thornton Cox 1972

RESIDENCES SECONDAIRES, Maison & Jardin 1972

RETIRE INTO THE SUN, *Cecil Chisholm,* Phoenix House 1961

SO YOU WANT A HOUSE IN SPAIN? *R. A. N. Dixon,* Collins 1964

THE HOMES OF AMERICA, *E. Pickering,* Bramhall House, New York 1961

VILLAS IN THE SUN, *Bernard Wolgensinger,* Charles E. Tuttle Co., Rutland 1971

WATERMILLS

BRITISH WATERMILLS, *L. Sysons,* Batsford 1965

OLD WATERMILLS AND WINDMILLS, *R. Thurston Hopkins*, 1930